Words of Wisdom

A Collection of Articles by
GURUDEV HAMSAH NANDATHA

Words of Wisdom

A Collection of Articles
by
GURUDEV HAMSAH NANDATHA

Path of Light Productions
Wasa, British Columbia

OTHER BOOK BY THE SAME AUTHOR

In the Presence of Truth - Discovering the Being Within ·
Volume 1

Library and Archives Canada Cataloguing in Publication

Hamsah Nandatha, Gurudev, author
        Words of wisdom : a collection of articles / by Gurudev
Hamsah Nandatha.

ISBN 978-0-9878418-2-7 (v. 1 : paperback)

    1. Spiritual life. I. Title.

BL624.H347 2016   204   C2016-900061-3

Published by: **PATH OF LIGHT PRODUCTIONS**
               P.O. Box 813, Cranbrook, BC, CANADA V1C 4J5
               www.pathoflightproductions.com

Foreword

Over the years, I have always been eager to read the next "Words of Wisdom" article in the periodical published by a remote community in the beautiful Canadian Rocky Mountains. Adjacent to this community is the remarkable Adi Vajra Shambhasalem Ashram of which the Venerable Gurudev Hamsah Nandatha is the Spiritual Leader. Gurudev wrote these articles as a generous contribution to the residents of the surrounding area.

I often thought how wonderful it would be if these writings could reach a much larger audience. They are written in such clear and understandable language, yet they contain profound and universal messages dating back to ancient times while being applicable to modern time. They provide practical advice that can be applied in daily life. They have a way of shifting perspective, broadening one's view and raising awareness. Most of all, they are written with Love, Light and Joy, offering guidance to those who want to be freed from uncontrollable thoughts and be immersed in a peaceful and creative state of mind.

I am therefore delighted that these articles have been made available through this book you are holding, and I hope they will connect you to the wonders of Creation, of which we are all an integral part.

May Gurudev Hamsah Nandatha's Words of Wisdom reach your heart and touch your soul and may you attain true Happiness.

OM OM OM

Vedhyas Sattviki
December 10th, 2015
Wasa, BC, Canada

Venerable Gurudev Hamsah Nandatha

TABLE OF CONTENTS

INTRODUCTION

Spiritual victory is not obtained by great sacrifices but rather by learning how to do the simple things of daily life with consciousness. This book is a collection of short texts written by Gurudev to guide seekers in the various aspects of daily life, showing how all aspects of human life can be lived with consciousness.

Through emotions, we tend to cover every moment that life brings us with layers of residual memories from our past and to clutter it with mental activities. By doing so, we can never live the fullness of the present, which is always filled with the Presence of the Divine. In this book, Gurudev guides the reader to find happiness and spiritual fulfillment through activities of daily life, so one can fully experience peace and harmony within.

In his book *In the Presence of Truth, Discovering the Being Within*, the Venerable Gurudev Hamsah Nandatha describes the process of Awakening like a roadmap, allowing anyone to journey through the process of the discovery of the Self. In this transition period between the Iron Age and the dawning Golden Age, Gurudev's Presence and Message is like a beacon guiding souls aspiring to be part of the next step in human evolution, going "*from the mental man to the Conscious Man*," as Gurudev says. But this journey begins right now, wherever you are, it begins with reading this book.

Hierophant Vedhyas Tashi Dorje
December 11th, 2015
Austin, TX, USA

THE ASHRAM

What is our Ashram in Wasa?

Traditionally, an ashram is a spiritual Hermitage directed by a spiritual teacher called a "Guru" belonging to an ancient lineage of Spiritual Masters. I am Gurudev Hamsah Nandatha, the Guru of the Adi Vajra Shambhasalem Ashram in Wasa. Here, I continue the Mission of my Master Shri Swami Hamsananda Sarawati, also called His Holiness the Lord Hamsah Manarah because of his high recognition as a Divine Incarnation by the most renowned Yogis and spiritual Figures of His time.

One of the most important Goals of the Teaching of my Master was rooted in Fraternity and Unity; to make all followers of different spiritual Traditions get closer to one another around the undeniable loving Principle of the Unity of God (the Divine). To do so, the Ashram is furnished with different statues representing the various Rays of the Divine as expected by the most prominent Religions on earth. In light of this, at the Ashram, the Cosmic Christ and the Buddha Maitreya are at the Universal Messiah's side symbolizing the perfect harmony between all Faces of the Divine. Christian, Jewish, Muslim and Hindu traditions all have their special place in our Ashram with a representation that is consistent with each respective Religion. Needless to say, the Ashram equally receives people coming from all creeds, traditions and Religions as long as they can respect the simple Principle of Oneness, the Unity of God. I regularly give Teachings concerning the diverse Spiritual Traditions existing among human beings and we sometimes have the joy of listening to other people talking about their Religion and how they turn their hearts toward God. Indian Swamis, Tibetan Monks, Christian Priests and Pastors as well as Rabbis and Teachers from any Tradition are always welcome to share with us their experience on the Path of Light and to enjoy the numerous Teachings and Meditation classes that are given here at the Ashram.

The main Teaching at the Ashram revolves around a few essential questions in life that cannot be ignored, such as: "What is the true purpose of existence?", "Who are we beyond our body and mind?", "What is the True Nature of one's Self?" and "How to achieve Self-Realization?" The practice of a logical and pragmatic inquiry through the Universal techniques of Yoga help aspirants to progressively remove the veil of ignorance in order to experience the true meaning of "Self-Realization".

It has been exactly 10 years since we opened the Ashram, which was the last will of my Spiritual Teacher before He passed away. The quality of the spiritual atmosphere here, my first book, and the kindness of our dedicated community have attracted more and more people from all over the world who have come to listen to Teachings on the wonderful adventure of their own consciousness. The flags of all of their countries stand proudly, high along the pathways of the beautiful gardens of the Ashram, reminding us that our world is becoming one vast village.

If you would like to learn more about our Ashram, or even come to visit, write to: International@adivajra.ca

I hope this will help you better understand the selfless and formidable work that we do at the Ashram to increase Fraternity, Unity and Love among humans.

HAPPINESS

We attract the Happiness we carry within

We live in an expanding universe, filled with the constant reactions of causes and effects that respond to and complement one another. These are constantly created, destroyed, and recreated, and they make us undergo an extraordinary evolutionary upsurge at every second.

Humanity cannot escape the law of cause and effect that Buddhism calls "karma", the action, the movement, and its repercussions in all aspects of our life.

Even alone, isolated in a cave at the top of a mountain, we are in constant interaction with the world in which we live. We always find ourselves in circumstances that correspond to what we carry within. We are surrounded by those whose traits we consciously or unconsciously carry inside of ourselves.

In a general view of humanity, and according to our tendencies, beliefs, desires and interests in life, we are linked by vibration, consciously or unconsciously, to types or groups of people with whom we interact directly or indirectly, whether we know them or not. As we say, "Birds of a feather flock together." This saying proves to be true at all levels in our relationship with the world.

One must also note that we attract to us situations and people that are both complementary and opposed to our own tendencies.

What we like the most in life puts us in contact with those

situations and people who reflect what we like. What we fear or reject the most attracts to us the people and circumstances that demonstrate our disgust or rejection. Thus, we are bound as much by our desires and what we accept as we are by our rejections, fears or denials. *What frustrations are needlessly created by a too frequently conflicted spirit!*

Most of the time, we look for happiness through our actions, words or thoughts as if it weren't already in us, while happiness should shine through all our modes of expression. Happiness is a state without conflict or contradiction. Happiness draws happiness!!!

Through our search for *eternal happiness*, we must realize that the state of happiness needs to be maintained, alive inside of us, and not conditional upon obtaining a new possession, a better situation, or living with a particular person or group of people.

What makes us happy is cultivating happiness, not limiting it to our projections and external demands.

Happiness is lived inside and shared with the world!

Happiness is a state of being!

Inevitably, we attract the happiness we carry within!

Happy or unhappy: it's our choice!

When we realize that a *state of happiness* is what we are looking for through everything we think, say, or do, we become more efficient at working toward this state in a cooperative and deliberate way instead of fighting against everything that runs contrary to it in our life.

We can either simply adopt the attitude of avoiding unhappiness, or work directly toward our happiness by making it the goal of our whole life. These two tendencies create a different impact on our psyche and our inner atmosphere, and hence on everything that concretely happens in our life.

Indeed, those who fight against unhappiness, sorrow, or fear associate psychically and energetically with those same destructive vibrations because they become permeable and receptive to all the circumstances corresponding to their inner focus. On the other hand, those who work only at being happy contribute to a state of happiness in themselves and in others. This is because, through a dynamic and joyous tendency, they associate with all who resemble them. Thus they constantly utilize of ways to maintain this state of happiness, whatever the circumstances in life.

The great goal of everyone is to live in a constant state of happiness. For this, it is essential to over-train ourselves to accept situations with realism, so as to develop a constructive and beneficial force of consciousness, whose direct and indirect impact permeates everything that comes in contact with us.

Santosha, or the art of facing all situations serenely, is the key to all liberation. No matter what we have done or not done, what we believe we are or not, we must decide, one day, to learn how to peacefully face whatever must be mastered or transformed within and around us.

The Love one carries within

We have all been children, and we know deep down inside how important love is. It is the very substance of life, the vital element without which a being cannot develop. We all aspire to love, to ever more love, and we never have enough. We deeply deplore living in a world that we experience as hostile, seemingly void of love. Without even talking about the wars and bloody conflicts that take place far away, our hearts are constantly cold amidst the difficult relationships we maintain with our close relatives, colleagues, or neighbors.

Without an inner harmony, which is experienced only in the unity of love, we feel the "pain of separation", which forces us to live in a feeling of inner isolation. We must, therefore, universally aspire to a single goal: to put an end to this separation and to recover the merging of love.

There are two kinds of love: *noble love*, which is directed toward ideals or beings who are worthy of veneration (called "Prema" in Sanskrit) and *ordinary love*, the affection felt for friends, siblings, a husband, wife, and so on, and even objects (called "Sneha"). In both cases, the emotion is the same, but the object is different. One should know that both kinds of love come into play in our hearts, but for some, one of them is predominant; that is the difference.

We see that everyone, by forming bonds of affection, tries to free themselves from feelings of isolation. However, the sages tell us that only the most noble love (Prema) can free us definitively from this terrible feeling of solitude. To find union with the world, we must allow our consciousness to expand.

It is only the superior form of love, inspired by a noble ideal, which will allow our minds to expand. When love is turned toward God, it becomes *bhakti*, or devotion. Those who love are then active; their love becomes dynamic; they do not expect to be loved by others. They are not beggars. They give, before thinking of receiving.

May Love be with you!

Don't say 'No' and be happy

From the moment you wake up in the morning until you wake up the next morning, whatever you do or think, I can assure you that you are looking for happiness. The pursuit of happiness for an ordinary mind is always related to things that are outside of you. The more people behave or situations unfold according to what you expect, the happier you are. But as you know, your expectations are rarely met because most of the time, the world does not fulfill your commands or desires. This is when you become frustrated, anxious, nervous, stressed, and angry. When the world does not correspond to what you expect, you are in an inner state of conflict, composed of feelings of disappointment or injustice. To be in contradiction with what the situations of daily life bring you is very childish. A true adult does not fight the reality of the world because he understands that the world cannot be otherwise at this moment. You cannot prevent situations that are happening right now. You cannot prevent people from being as they are right now. In other words, you cannot say 'no' to what happens, because it *is* happening. No matter how frustrated you are, what is happening in your life right now cannot be changed. It will change on the course of time but not now; right now, everything is as it is, that's it! Do not deny what is!

When you are in conflict with the world, even your very small personal world, you cannot be happy, because happiness is an inner state without conflict or contradiction. When you have no conflicts or contradictions, then you are happy, and it seems to you that the world is beautiful and at peace; as it should always be.

How do you enter in conflict with the world? It is when you do not accept the world anymore, when you don't like a situation and you say 'no' to it. Through this revelation that I'm giving you, happiness is within your reach. The key to everlasting happiness is: stop denying; stop saying 'no' to the world. In reality, you can never say 'no' to what happens; the only choice you have is to fully accept it, while remaining very careful about your old habits of saying 'no' and denying reality.

Saying 'no' through everything that you dislike is a crime against your own happiness and that of others. Saying 'yes' to what happens, whether you like it or not, protects happiness within yourself and others. So, remember that each time you say 'no', you are on the verge of being unhappy, and then change your attitude by saying 'yes'. This way, you will be able to improve situations or relationships, and you will maintain the feeling of freedom brought by the true happiness that resides within you. If you are uncomfortable and unhappy, it is always because there is something that you deny; so, don't do it anymore!

Don't say 'no', say 'yes' to what the Divine Force brings you at every moment and you will be happy forever. Whatever happens, you have the power to overcome it and you will.

May these words of practical Wisdom help you in your daily life: don't say 'no' and be happy.

What's next for you to be fulfilled and totally happy?

What are you doing right now to obtain a glimpse of happiness? What are your plans in order to be really happy... forever? Have you ever noticed how many things we do in life with the expectation of being endlessly happy and complete? Let's take your own life as an example: what are you doing right now with the sole (yet hidden) desire of being happy and problem-free? It could be, "*Oh, Honey! Let's organize a nice lunch with the family; the kids are coming this weekend.*" or "*Darling! Fall is here now, let's spend winter in Mexico; it is so much livelier and warmer there!*" It could also be, "*It's late, let's have a nice supper and watch TV all evening!*" or "*Let's drink hot chocolate, walk the dog or repaint the living room; let's go to the movies, take a warm shower or phone your best friend*", and so on! No matter what you do, it is to be happier and, in the end, to be totally happy and fulfilled! You crave happiness, peace and full satisfaction!

To be happy! Oh, God! What have you not done for this? You have defied all obstacles, all impediments. Most of all, you have put all your energy, all your faith, all your hope into it, and you will continue to do so for the rest of your life! But what kind of balance sheet are you left with after all these years of fighting for happiness and fulfillment?

Have you ever reflected upon the nature of the happiness you are looking for? What do you need today to be happy? What's next? Are you really going to be completely and totally happy with what you plan to do? Or is it simply, for you, the sad acceptance that no one can be happy forever so it is better to take as many glimpses of happiness as we can before dying?

Happiness is one of the most important words in the Yoga

Sadhana Practice. Happiness refers to bliss or "Ananda", absolute fulfillment, total completeness. For us Yogis, happiness is a state of being which should be achieved from within. No matter what you add to your life in order to be happy, none of it carries happiness in and of itself. Happiness is only a concept that you project upon people, objects, or situations. You might hope to find happiness with someone, something or in certain circumstances, while the same conditions could be a source of discomfort for someone else. For example, you may think you'll be happy basking under the sun on the beach, but this might not be the case for someone who hates sand and summer heat. No matter what adds up to your version of happiness, it is just a play of your mind; nothing outside of you contains happiness. *You are the sole carrier of your happiness*!

When wisdom grows within you through various experiences in life, you realize that the happiness you've been looking for from the start of this incarnation has in fact been produced and projected everywhere you want by none other than *you*.

What if, rather than expecting to be happy by adding something external to you, you realized that you could be happy right now and forever with what is? In other words, why only try to be happy later, when you can absolutely be happy right now? By avoiding being in contradiction with what happens in your life, you become one with reality and the feelings that arise from this are fulfillment, oneness and completeness. You do not need anything else other than what is; you need only to project happiness on what is *as it is* in order to experience happiness here and now!

Rather than complicating everything for a little bit of happiness later, may all of you seek happiness right now for no reason!

POSITIVE THINKING

The Joy of being responsible for one's own life

Many situations in life leave us with a feeling of heaviness and anxiety, like a little something that is constantly missing inside. We often feel like a victim of situations. It's a sort of pressure that weighs heavily on the heart and mind. That is when we must aspire to simply be ourselves, in a state of peace and joy at each moment. We are made for Happiness, but are we looking for it, directly and sincerely? Have we learned the true nature of happiness? What if we simply carry it within?

The universal wisdom of integral yoga teaches us that humans are beings of transition; that they constantly evolve while seeking their absolute Nature, their true Nature.

There is an inner Self that we must take the time to discover. It exists beyond daily worries, beyond thoughts and emotions. It is more powerful and wonderful than anything life on the surface has to offer. The true inner Self is the source of all plenitude, while what we believe to be oneself at the surface of thoughts is the source of conflicts and contradictions. We are as much responsible for our joys as for our sorrows; nothing happens by chance.

The saying goes, *"Tell me what you think, I'll tell you who you are"*, and I often add for the aspirants at the Ashram, *"Tell me what emotions you carry inside, I will tell your future."* All sorts of things happen inside and outside of us, but what do we do with what simply happens? We often distort situations according to our own viewpoint, turning them into something completely different from what really happened. We bring on to ourselves all that happens in our life through our own doing, directly or indirectly, consciously or unconsciously! Every cause produces an effect!

Everyone should see themselves as responsible for everything that happens in their own inner or outer life. There is, in everything, a law of interdependence according to which every action, thought, emotion and word, as insignificant as it may seem, inevitably produces a related effect, sooner or later. Everything is energy; all things are related!

The past cannot be changed; only the present can, and the way you react to it can bring about a happy future. You can only be happy by learning "*Santosha*", the art of living without contradictions, without conflicts with the reality of your own life. No matter what troubles you have at this moment, this moment is not the bearer of your trouble; in fact, nothing threatens you. So, come back to the center of yourself, rely on your true inner Self, breathe, and return to the sense of calm, peace and serenity within so you can stop falsifying and altering reality. Every situation has its right solution!

When you realize you are responsible for everything that happens in your life, it becomes easy to create the state of happiness to which you aspire, and to communicate it to everybody around you!

May all good things be granted to you for your spiritual Evolution!

What do you promote?

In the spiritual practices of India or Tibet, the term "Karma" does not designate only bad situations that happen in your life, but all actions that create any consequences.

If you want to understand karma, you have to understand the meaning of action. What is an action? An action is everything that comes from thinking, talking, acting, breathing, watching, or hearing. All your senses produce an action.

From action comes reaction. You hear something, and you react. You say something, and someone else will react, even if it is in a positive way. You see something, and you react. We live like this all the time. So now, if you understand the principle of action, you understand that no matter what is happening to you, the way you are going to react will have an impact on your surroundings. It could be visible or extremely subtle, existing only at the level of energy, but the effect will go on and on.

When you understand the principle of action, you can understand the principle of Unity. If you are disharmonious, you will, through your reactions, promote disharmony. If you seek harmony and happiness, through your reactions, you will promote harmony and unity.

May all of you enjoy carrying out harmonious actions to promote harmonious reactions in your daily life.

Which wolf do you feed?

Universal wisdom can be found anywhere you go. Not far from us here in North America, there is a very wise nation of Native Americans called the Cherokee Nation. From them, I have learned a true story of wisdom, which is worthy of the teachings by the most famous Sages, as inspiring as the teachings of Christ and the Buddha.

Here is this powerful Cherokee story:

A Cherokee elder was talking to his grandson: "*In every man, there is a terrible fight -- a fight between two wolves.*

One is evil: he is fear, anger, envy, greed, arrogance, self-pity, resentment, and deceit.

The other one is good: he is joy, serenity, humility, confidence, generosity, truth, gentleness, and compassion."

The child asked, "*Grandfather, which wolf will win?*"

The elder looked him in the eye and replied: "*The one you feed.*"

The meaning of this story is that the development of good character depends on the choices you make in everyday life. All is a question of knowing which 'wolf' you want to feed, because, to feed the 'good wolf', you need to train yourself to be aware of what you think, what you say, and what your true motivation is in what you do! If you want to live a happy life and share your joy with everyone, then put all your energy in feeding the liberating virtues of the 'good wolf' that you are.

Thanks to the Cherokee people!

Be careful what you wish for!

The word "Karma" means action, and an action corresponds to the production of a certain amount of energy needed to provoke a change in a particular situation in order to achieve a specific goal. It is common to refer to action as occurring only when we move or do something with our hands; but an action is also induced through what we say. When you pronounce certain words, you produce sounds that mean something for those who are listening to them. Therefore, what we say also creates action. If you try to assist someone in parking a big truck into a narrow space by instructing the driver while you are outside the vehicle and if the driver trusts your vocal information, then through the precision of your words you can easily steer a 10-wheeler without moving a muscle. An entire country can enter into war through the simple exchange of words, able to set thousands of soldiers into motion. By the lack of control of your speech, you can alter your own destiny and the destiny of others. In yoga we say that the control of one's tongue is essential to fostering Unity and Harmony.

Now, it is interesting to reflect upon the driving motivations behind what we say. *Why do you say what you say? Why do you want your words to be heard, accepted and respected by others?* It is because, through your words, you communicate your intentions and hope for others to respect, love and recognize you as a presence representing a certain authority in life. By communicating, you try to avoid falling into oblivion in the minds of others. No matter what you say, you say it because, behind every word that you choose to use, there is a more or less conscious desire, wish, or demand that you hope will be fulfilled.

Before saying anything, there is a production of thought, and you think what you think not because you have decided to think about it, but because it has been imposed upon you by a conscious or unconscious desire. You act because you think, and you think because you have emotions and desires. Emotions and desires that are not consciously perceived by you only make you *react* according to your past and not act according to the present situation.

When you act, speak or think, you produce an energy of intention. This energy is tinged, as it is oriented according to what you want, wish, hope for, or expect. The production of the energy of intention is called "Vritti" in Yoga. In the Sanskrit language, "*Yoga Chitta Vritti Nirodha*" means that 'Yoga is the practice of removing any and all modifications of the mind.' Once the energy of intention (Vritti) is produced through your desires, it will spread all around you, and try to modify the subtle energetic and physical worlds according to what you deeply wish for.

In other words, thinking is already provoking an action, a transformation in your life. The smallest thought, almost unperceived by you, will have an irreversible impact on your life according to the nature of its emotion or desire of origin. So be careful what you wish for through all the scenarios automatically and unwillingly produced by your mind. Nothing happens by accident; everything that happens to you corresponds to you. You will always find yourself in situations that correspond to your own thought processes.

By being aware of the production of your mind and by verifying whether your thoughts are beneficial to others and to yourself, you can easily change your destiny, the destiny of those you love and in fact, from right where you are, the destiny of the entire world.

May all of you learn to think according to the true reality, in a positive way, fully understanding what is really necessary and what you really want to achieve: the state of true happiness that you deeply seek through everything you do. These elements are essential in the practice of our Integral Yoga leading directly to Self-Realization.

Through our Awareness, we can all become the Artisans of our common human Destiny!

REALITY

Reality is within us

What is reality? Is reality your vision of the chocolate you covet? When you have problems, when you're in conflict, when you see unhappy people, is it reality or not?

In truth, everything you consider as good or bad, the entire world of sensations, is just your mental invention. It's your mind that creates it. Nothing that exists in this world is absolutely or automatically good or bad. *That's impossible!*

It is important to discover what reality is for your own mind, from your individual point of view. Consider a chair, for example. You say: "*I see that this chair exists.*" But in fact, this chair did not exist for you until you came close enough to see it. When you look at something, inevitably a mental energy is sent into the atmosphere, and then you say: "*I see a chair, this chair. It is this, it is that!*" Even though your dualistic mind perceives the chair as exterior to you, it is in fact a part of your mind's nature; the chair and your consciousness are united.

In the same way, it is your mental energy that makes things appear good or bad. Everything we perceive is created by our mind; nothing exists externally, or is fixed in one way or another.

Develop clairvoyance and see reality *as it is*

Clairvoyance is a gift that allows us to perceive matter beyond its mere appearance in order to serve as an instrument of the Divine. To see beyond appearances, we must aspire to cease accepting only what situations and people appear to be; to live with what happens at every present moment, without distorting situations according to our preferences, and to be more a witness than a constant actor in our lives!

We must also step back within, and not run away or become indifferent to situations and people. True clairvoyance is within everyone's reach. It requires one to be even more involved in real life, just less dependent on appearances and views as an ego or a personality.

Those who have developed true clairvoyance see through the eyes of Universality, and are not subject to the interpretations of the mind. They have developed the sense of Unity with the Cosmo-Universal Divine Force, and they therefore, see things in their true context, not according to the imaginary wishes of the mind.

To become a clear-sighted Being, one must train to enter into an ever-deepening constant Peace. One must also learn to feel the forces in action as they are, and not as one imagines them, nor as one likes them or fears them. Natural clairvoyance is in fact a totally spontaneous perception, which causes one to feel first and consequently, to know.

A clairvoyant being has a peaceful mind and a pure and joyous heart. The Divine Force moves through him and he is only the receiver of the elements he perceives for the good of every being he meets. The Servant of Light has a duty to develop clairvoyance for the service of Humanity. His degree of clairvoyance depends on his Unity with the Divine Force, which is One.

May the Light of the Almighty illuminate your path at every moment of the day and night!

See *the* facts rather than *your* facts

To open oneself to what is does not mean to accept it in a condescending way and say, "*Yes, that is very good.*" Rather, it is to be receptive to the situation beyond any judgment. To **accept** implies that we are in agreement with and hold as entirely true what is happening. To be **receptive** to the situation, on the other hand, is to neither accept nor deny anything. It consists of saying: "*This seems to be this way at the moment, but let's have a closer look.*" So, to **accept** is a way of being condescending, while to be receptive consists of keeping an open mind to see what is happening. When we are receptive, what we see is considerably different from appearances.

Most of us react to something that appears to be negative with a reflex of negativity in ourselves: "*I don't feel like accepting this or opening myself to the confusion or conflict that is happening in me. I cannot be receptive to the uneasiness that this creates in me.*" However, if we are able to open up a little to the confusion in our mind, we see that it is not all that confused, because once we examine the feeling, the ego-self no longer identifies with the bewilderment. Then our experience becomes a mere observation of the uneasiness we carry within! By being just a little bit observant of this uneasiness within, we realize that it is not that painful. We see that our pain was equaled only by our will to resist what **is** or **was**, which opposed our ideas about how things 'should' be.

When we are able to open ourselves clearly and honestly to what **is**, we become masters of the facts and we eliminate our subjectivity, and with it, the source of our uneasiness. We see certain things that have ordinary causes and others which originate from our own way of interfering. Thus, we see more clearly what we can do in relation to what **is**, rather than wasting energy fighting against it. It is not a question of fighting against the world, but to get over *our* world, and to appreciate life in its reality.

May your world be in peace with *the* world.

Are you *that* special?

The main reason why we are so obsessed with our own lives is because we have not equalized ourselves with others. We think we are different from others, but in reality everybody is the same. Everyone wants to be happy and to avoid suffering. Yet, we keep everybody else outside of our frame of reference, avoiding inquiry into others; thinking only of ourselves. We want to do well so we think, "*I need to do this, I need to be happy, I need to solve this problem.*" Others become totally incidental in such preoccupation. Self-obsession causes us to mistakenly perceive others as not equal; as less important.

Who has been leading us to all the unwanted trouble and suffering? It is the self-cherishing mind, the self-centered thoughts that have taken possession of our mind. It is an attitude in which we consider ourselves to be more important and better than everybody else, or where we feel we need to achieve more than everybody else—whether it is a possession, happiness or getting rid of problems. This attitude is the cause of all our problems.

There are seven billion humans on this planet, as well as innumerable insects, birds and other sentient beings. Like us, they dislike suffering and just want to be happy. The big difference between ourselves and others is in scale: the amount and weight of the suffering of all other beings is massive in comparison to the weight of suffering that lies on one person. It is totally meaningless to be constantly obsessed with ourselves, when in fact we are not the most important. When we realize that it is the weight of collective suffering that is most important, we will think and meditate on it, and we will equalize ourselves with others.

All goodness and happiness arises when we wish others to be happy. Everything that runs smoothly and well in our lives comes from cherishing others. Whatever exists requires causes and conditions—it doesn't happen randomly. The same goes for our happiness. When we cherish others, we are generous and we do not get angry with others—we practice patience, morality and non-harm.

It is entirely up to us. If we don't want to suffer, we have to cherish others.

May you be a dynamic source of harmony all around you and then for yourself.

Pragmatism to the rescue: the art of seeing the facts *as they are*!

A Sage once said: *"You will never see a successful man happy; it is always the happy man who is successful."*

Are you happy or are you just holding on to your life with moroseness and regrets or fear, conflicts, contradiction, indignation or a hope for better days?

No matter what is in front of you at the moment, it is a challenge for your true presence that witnesses it. Do not be opposed to situations; learn how to accompany them. Tell yourself: *"No matter what is happening, it is happening and I must face it with neutral vision in order to make all the right decisions."*

You cannot change what has happened or what is happening; you can only flow with it and do what is necessary to improve the situation as much as possible.

Do not let your emotions distort or aggravate the situation; it is simply what it is, even if it was unexpected. No matter what you are going through right now, it will pass, because nothing lasts forever.

If you want to be happy and efficient in all situations, always act and react in a non-personal way. Do not let negative emotions steal your inner ability to be free from personal reactions. If you feel tense because of personal emotions, do not let them distract you from the simple facts. Even if the world, constructed by your ego, is attacked, do not make it personal, as you are not in the real world to grow a bigger ego, rather you are here to get rid of it and to live in freedom as your true Self, in Unity with the Divine Force.

As soon as you are willing to face any situation as it is, in an impersonal way, you will immediately feel freer, more relaxed, more lucid and happier. You will start being in control of yourself.

Peacefully accompany what is happening, act to be more and more harmonious by using pragmatism as a shield. In dealing with any situation, make it impersonal and instantly you will be more peaceful. From peace comes clarity of mind, from clarity of mind come righteous actions, and from righteous actions comes harmony and happiness for all!

May every moment of your life be accompanied by your impersonal state of mind.

Clarifying your perception is possible

Any event happens because it *cannot not* happen, and if you really understand this, with all of your intelligence, you will become less and less indignant, and you will increasingly accept what happens rather than rejecting or denying it. One must reflect upon the following truth: "*one always attracts to oneself the events of one's life*", and this is true, no matter what they are. In fact, consciously or unconsciously, you attract to you all the events of your life. Even more, you attract to you what you are afraid of as much as what you desire. It is not easy to understand this, especially when one goes through adverse situations that the mind qualifies as unjust. If the word acceptance seems inaccessible to you, then replace it by *seeing and recognizing what is as it is*. What you like or dislike never changes the nature of situations. Even if your mind makes you believe that your emotions are related to a situation and are part of the situation, it is never true! The situation is always brand new and your emotions are old emotions that come from your past. If you train yourself to catch your mind in the process of covering reality with ancient emotions that you already carried within you before the event, you will realize that the event is just the event, and that a part of you deforms it through the weight of your past. In all cases, the event remains as it is and, to respond to it properly, you must remove from the facts everything that your mind makes up about them. This is valid for any situation and any relationship that you can have with anyone.

To act in a just and perfect way, keep your attention on yourself to see what kind of emotion that is unrelated to the situation rises in you. Then put it aside and focus your attention on the situation, or the person in front of you. Do this to remain present and really perceive the facts as they are without deforming them through what you want or do not want, like or dislike.

From there, you will maintain a clear perception of every-thing that simply happens and you will be astonished by your ability to handle everything smoothly and peacefully, no matter what.

Try it every time you can remember, and you will see mira-cles unfold in your life.

May the Divine Consciousness assist you in all the challenges of life.

What about your resolutions?

Deep resolutions require a sharp understanding and an untamable will, two elements that grow side by side as one progresses. If you have a clear understanding of your goal, your spirit strives to attain this ideal with an untamable will. For an advanced yogi, there is no distinction between understanding and will. However, for a less advanced aspirant, these two notions appear to be separate attainments, and self-effort must be applied toward developing both.

Beware of superficial resolutions based on the ego.

Many people tend to make superficial resolutions that are based on egoistic illusion and which, when they are kept, bring very little benefit, and often result in greater egoistic illusion. For example, if you resolve to walk a long distance barefoot and you achieve this feat, you might become so conceited that for the rest of your life all you talk about is your courage. In the long run, it would be better to waiver along the way and interrupt your walk. It would make you much humbler.

Similarly, suppose that either for the sake of your health or that of your will, you resolve not to eat sugar for ten days. During the whole ten days, whenever you see other people eating sugar, you will think only of sugar and you will count the days until your vow is fulfilled. The tenth day finally comes and you greedily eat vast amounts of sugar! Such are the resolutions of an unreflective person.

A yogi, on the other hand, uses moderation in making such resolutions. He does not resolve to stop eating sugar, but rather to reduce the quantity he eats. If you realize that sugar isn't good for you and that you shouldn't eat so much of it, you will begin to regulate it more day by day. Similarly, if you realize that you shouldn't talk so much, you will begin to control your speech, little by little, no matter how much you hesitate in doing so. In this way, you don't even realize you are disciplining yourself.

You should develop a lifestyle that is highly disciplined, but not develop, at the same time, the burden that you are practicing great discipline. Discipline your personality, and take pleasure in having all your energy, talents and resources organized. To others, it may seem a rigorous process, but for you, it will be a source of joy. As long as you are able to transform a disciplinary process into a natural process, you will have no trouble keeping your resolutions. But if your discipline is rigid, your resolutions will create tension and will most likely be broken.

Hoping this will help you hold on to your resolutions in a joyous way. I wish for you to succeed in finding the best resolution for you at this point in your life.

Do you perceive reality rightfully?

Most people believe that what they think, say, hear or do is based in reality when really it is only a response to their limited perception of it. How many times have you realized after thinking, saying, interpreting or doing something, that you were in fact completely wrong? Then, in reflecting upon it, you were able to realize how deformed your interpretation of the situation was, with all of your exaggerated opinions or convictions?

In the universal Advaita (Non-Duality) yogic tradition, there is an interesting story, which was told to me by my Guru about how wrong we can be in our interpretation of reality.

At twilight, in a small village in India, a young woman screams at the sight of a dangerous snake in the middle of her path. All the villagers run to her side and begin questioning why the snake is rolled up around itself. *"What is it doing here? It is a bad omen! What kind of snake is it? Look, it's moving!"* Some say, *"It must be poisonous, we should throw stones to kill it!"* After a few minutes of throwing stones at the snake, they presume it must be dead. A courageous man, armed with a long stick, ventures up to the snake and attempts to touch it with the tip of his staff. He carefully pushes it, confirming the snake's death. Catching the snake around his stick, he brings it back to the light and says, *"Oh! Look, it is not a snake at all! It is only a rope, which must have been left by a fisherman along his travels! We have mistaken the rope for a snake."*

In this example, it is easy to see that there was no snake at all but only a rope from the start. This story illuminates the mind's constant deforming of reality through the fallacious process of unjustified comparison. In the practice of Sadhana (the conscious work for inner spiritual awakening) we quickly learn that comparing *what is* with *what was* often leads to aberrations and false representations of reality.

If you have a tendency to believe that your mind expresses the true reality to your consciousness, then it is time for you to become the witness of all the misleading aberrations of your mind. You must understand that it is always through your mind that situations are exaggerated, leading to inappropriate reactions. Then it is important to recognize the difference between facts that comprise reality and the illusory representation of reality that is projected by your mind.

Stay with the facts, and not according to what you like or dislike, want or don't want, but according to the true reality without any preferences. In doing so, you will be astonished by how quiet, balanced and calm you can become in any situation of life, no matter what. Through lucidity and objectivity, life becomes as clear as a pure diamond.

Do not cherish your opinions or your certainties; rather observe your mind and question its objectivity!

May happiness, clarity and lucidity be the guardian of your harmony within and with others.

CONSCIOUSNESS

Are you aware of yourself?

The mind is very quick to create alternate versions of situations a person faces each day. The mind is mostly made up of two things: desires and fear. This is so because of the accumulation of previous experiences that one has had in life that have left traces within oneself under the form of impressions. These impressions are in fact emotions that compel one to wish reality to be different from what it is according to what one expects, wants, likes or dislikes.

In other words, the mind deforms reality and prevents one's consciousness from perceiving situations or other people as they are. The mind colors reality and transforms it into *what should be* rather than seeing *what simply is*. When someone speaks to you rudely, your mind creates a second problem, which is, "*this should not happen.*" If you come back to the reality of what is happening within you, you will realize that even your anger cannot remove the fact that someone has spoken to you under the influence of their own emotions, which also deform reality and make them say rude things.

When you lose consciousness of your presence and, hence, what is going on within you, the mind digs into your memories to describe the current reality according to what kind of impressions have marked you in the past, at which point you lose the ability to agree with the reality of what is simply happening in front of you.

To avoid deforming the reality of events in your daily life

as often as possible, put your attention on what kind of emotion rises up within you at that moment. You may discover that you are overwhelmed by fear, insecurity, anger, regret, jealousy, envy, and the like. And once you are conscious of this element, you will not allow your mind to dramatize or deform any fact that is actually happening. Peace of mind will be with you and you will then act appropriately!

What happens, happens: you cannot fight against what is happening; you first have to accept it, then deal with it with a clear mind.

As soon as you lose awareness of yourself, you stop existing in your own life, and you lose the ability to perceive what is happening *as it is*. Then your mind can replace a simple fact by a nightmare that does not truly exist. It is always something that is just happening.

If you want to be calm and secure so you can act justly, remain aware of yourself and of what exists in you that will, if you let it, transform a simple fact into a drama.

May this message of wisdom be of great help at every moment of your life, especially when you meet adversity.

Do you often disappear from your life?

Have you ever felt that what you think about all day long is not what you want to think, but something that is imposed on you? For example, when you follow a wild scenario in your head while driving your car, even though nothing of what you think about relates to the present moment?

Have you ever had the impression that what you say is not the fruit of a conscious reflection, but the result of an impulsive and instinctive reflex? For example, if someone speaks rudely to you, and you immediately respond aggressively, as if you were possessed by ancient dark forces called "emotions"?

Have you noticed that what you do is often done without being conscious of it? For example, when you drive from one place to another, and once at your destination, you are unable to remember what happened along the way.

If this is the case, don't worry; you are not crazy! With a little bit of honesty, everyone can answer positively to these questions and say: *"Most of the time I don't choose to think what I think about. Most of the time, I don't know what I am saying. Most of the time, I even don't know what I am doing."*

The reason for such a lack of awareness is that, between your consciousness (the real *you*) and what is happening in reality, your mind plays the role of an illusionist. In yoga, we learn how to make the distinction among one's consciousness, the autonomous activity of one's mind, and the reality of every event happening in one's life.

In other words, as soon as you lose awareness of what you are comprised of at any moment, you also lose the ability to remain conscious of the illusions and distractions created by your mind through your memories, expectations and emotions. In fact, by losing awareness of your true presence, you become a puppet of the mechanical mind. You disappear before your own eyes as if you ceased to exist for varying periods of time throughout the day. It's as if you think, talk and do without even being aware of existing!

To avoid being the victim of this lack of awareness and unwanted thoughts, words and actions, it is important to frequently ask yourself these simple questions: "*Am I conscious of what I am thinking about right now? Is it really what I want to think about? Am I conscious of where I am right now? Am I fully aware of what I am saying? Am I aware of what I am doing? Is this really what should be said or done?*"

From there, you will quickly gain control of your mind and of yourself and, from this will arise the perception of things that a distracted human being cannot perceive. Ultimately, through this simple exercise of self-awareness at every moment, you will realize the power contained in the growing peacefulness within you.

Don't let your mind make you disappear from your life! Practice awareness and vigilance without tension and you will find the right solution for every situation that you encounter.

What covers your consciousness

In the spirit of Yoga Sadhana, or spiritual inquiry, the Yogi strives to experience his or her true nature beyond all appearance in the physical world. Most teachings of the great spiritual Masters from all spiritual traditions explain that we are not just this crude and perishable body, nor are we only the story of this life, but rather we are the expression of a Superior Intelligence, a Supreme Consciousness, called God or the Divine.

Imagine for a moment that what you believe about yourself, even what you know about yourself, has nothing to do with who you really are!!! By the simple will of your consciousness, you can instantaneously become the observer of your body. Since you cannot be the very thing you are observing, then you must ask *who is the one observing the body?* You can also observe your mind and the thought forms as they are developing in your head. Ask yourself, *who is the one within who is able to observe these thoughts?* If you want, you can even become the observer of your own emotions, of your mood; you can be the witness of your own inner atmosphere. And again as you witness, ask yourself, *who is the one observing these emotions and strange sensations that create this mood?*

We have been raised as if we were only our body, thoughts and emotions, as if our name, form, and even the story of our life were the entire composition of what we know to be ourselves. But when you think about it more deeply, if at any moment we can become the witness of anything that is happening within us, then the essential question concerns the very nature of *you* as a pure observer.

During the public meditations or Teachings at the Ashram, I share the breathtaking story of the Adventure of Consciousness, revealing what its true nature is, how it has been hidden and mixed up with the mind, and most importantly, how to have a daily experience not of *being* a body, but rather of *using* a body. I share concretely with you all how it is absolutely possible to experience that you are not your mind, but rather a free Consciousness. It is just that this consciousness has more often than not been used and tricked by the imposed thought processes of the mind.

On the Path of Yoga Sadhana, laden with the renowned spiritual question *"who am I?"*, it is interesting to discover that the true spirit of a Yogi is comprised of extreme logic and pragmatism. There isn't much room for dreamers on the path of Self-Realization! So, by discovering a clear logical explanation about your condition in this life, it becomes evident that your consciousness and its Divine Nature have simply been covered by different "layers" identified as your body, emotions, and thought processes. By learning how to become the witness of these different coverings of the Consciousness, you progressively free it from all limitations and all sufferings.

Beyond your body and your mind, there is the true "you", the Conscious Self and this discovery gives you another life, a true life in the real world.

May the passion for Truth guide you toward the Unity of the Divine within.

Are we good citizens?

As my own Spiritual Teacher, His Holiness the Lord Hamsah Manarah, used to do, I often remind all the spiritual Seekers at the Ashram not to forget to be excellent Citizens in their daily activities. What would be the point of following a Messiah, a Prophet, a Saint or a living Embodiment of God, if we forgot our responsibilities toward the physical world? How could one claim to serve the Divine and be a true Disciple of any great Soul if one forgets to improve the situation of the world by becoming a true living example of the Teaching of one's own Master?

All the good qualities and virtues contained in the Universal Declaration of Human Rights that are promoted and defended by the United Nations, are commonly understood as inalienable fundamental rights to which the person is inherently entitled simply by being human. These rights, virtues, qualities and duties are inherent in all human beings regardless of their nation, region, language, religion, ethnic origin or any other status.

Where do they come from, these Universal Rights and Duties that are the basis of any true Democracy and the expression of advanced civilizations? They come from the good sense of highly Spiritual Beings who reflected upon the human condition and discovered how important it is to unite all nations of the world around Universal Human Virtues and Qualities of Heart.

If we want to benefit from what is contained in the Universal Declaration of Human Rights, we need to develop and express in our daily life a profound understanding and acceptance of others, because we place these indispensable qualities as defining the very nature of a Genuine Human Citizen of planet Earth.

To be a true Citizen is to be a part of something very Precious: an important Member of the Human Community, someone who counts because s/he makes the world better by his or her own presence. *Are you a good citizen? Are we good citizens? Do we make the world better? Or do we make it worse?* We are not just the citizens of our country because we can vote; we are also citizens of our planet and of the entirety of creation. If we believe that God (*the Divine Consciousness*) is at the origin of creation and participates in it at every level, then we are also Citizens of the Divine! The Divine Principle is a principle of Love, and the principle of Love is a principle of Inclusion, a principle of Unification, a principle of Oneness. Therefore, to be a good Citizen is also to fight against our own egoism and selfishness and to act kindly, simply for the harmony of all of Humanity.

As you know, life does not always fulfill our expectations. Life is life, and what we qualify as good or bad is often a selfish point of view. In life, there is only what happens and, through the acceptance and recognition of what simply happens, we must protect the Unity of our "citizen-hood". What someone does in terms of thoughts, speech, and actions affects all the citizens around them. Your uncontrolled anger at home, as insignificant as it can seem, will subtly damage the Unity of the entire Nation or of our global Human family.

If you consider yourself a spiritual person, you can practice your spiritual precepts by improving your positive action in the world as a good citizen who takes care of all the members of the big family of our Humanity. My Revered Guru once told me that "*A single good Action made by a single excellent Citizen can beneficially change the Destiny of all of Humanity at every second*", and this assertion has been proven right. Mother Teresa, Nelson Mandela, Mahatma Gandhi and so many other unknown great Citizens of this world have shown us the Path leading toward a better world. It is now up to us to do our part!

May we all be excellent Citizens of our country, of the world and the entire Creation that is certain to contain billions and billions of inhabited planets.

The Power of the Use of Silence in Thinking, Speaking and Acting

We rarely realize how damaging our unnoticed emotional impulses of thinking, talking and acting as instinctive reactions to what is happening can be. Free will is a mere illusion when one realizes that one does not think, but is being thought by one's "automatic mind"; that one does not speak but rather is compelled to say what pops up in one's head; and that one does not choose to act but constantly reacts according to one's past.

You have not chosen what you think; it is imposed upon you by your unconscious mind. You have not chosen to say what you say; it comes by itself without your conscious consent. You haven't chosen vanilla ice cream; your past desire for it has made the choice for you and you are unaware because you have not yet been trained to see this.

Following the mind has become a part of us, so we are convinced that we make our own choices. For example, you have unconscious memories associated with the color blue, and when someone asks you, *"What is your favorite color?"* you immediately answer, *"Blue is my favorite color!"* Every human being is programmed by their past. We do every single thing according to our past, not according to the present. Unless we develop awareness of this, we will remain the slave of our past, unable to live in the real world, in the present moment as it is. From the beginning, we have all been tricked by our identification with the mind; we accept everything that pops up into our head as true and real. Don't believe everything your mind creates; it is an illusion, a simple reflection of what is real, a single angle of vision in your mental world!

The use of the Power of Silence is an essential Yogic technique that consists of creating silence before any action in order to cease being used by your emotional past. As fast as possible, stop and observe the true motivation of any action and correct it right away.

1. **Thought process**: Silence your mind by observing what is being thought in your head right now. Have you willingly chosen that thought? Is it beneficial for you and others or is it damaging to think like this? Is what you are thinking about in touch with the present moment? If not, then correct the mind's situation by choosing to think only about what is positive and favorable for you and others at that moment.

2. **Speech process**: Before saying anything, silence your use of words by observing the true motivation of what you were about to say. Is what you were about to say true or untrue, ignorant or egoistic according to your personal viewpoint? Is your motivation to be more loved and recognized; to impress others? Or is it to respond adequately to what must be said to promote harmony?

3. **Action process**: Silence or refrain from carrying out any impulsive action. Become conscious of what you are about to do to ensure it corresponds to the necessity of the moment, without greed or personal benefit, but rather for the joy of doing only what is right. Rather than reacting, simply act, which is to do only what is necessary without any attachment to the past or the future.

These three manners of using the Power of Silence can help anyone remain in control and efficient in the real world, without being impaired by frustration, guilt or remorse. It is the best and most efficient way to destroy all Karma of suffering within one's heart and in the hearts of those you love.

May these powerful practices be at your service anytime you want to return to Peace and Harmony in your life.

Do you take the time to just *Be*?

In a world where everything moves so fast, where communication is everywhere, where everything is constantly asking you to do something, there is virtually no place or time to be anymore. You think you are being, but you are not; you are just *doing*. Doing is the state of most people all the time. We have gotten lost in the *doing*. We have lost ourselves in this excess of doing and in this unstoppable and constant urge to do in the hope of one day doing what will finally make us truly happy.

Have you ever reflected upon the reason, the very reason behind everything you do? *Really, why do you do what you do? What do you hope for? What is the expectation behind what you are doing, no matter what it is?* This series of questions may sound strange, especially because you have no time to ask yourself these questions. But if you pay close attention, you will realize that you don't really know why you are doing all that you do. You don't just *do*, you are constantly *compelled to do*. It is as though you were thinking: *"What's the next thing I'm going to do to forget who I am?"* and you remain unhappy despite of all you do, because you don't really know who you are. If you don't know who you are, how can you really know what you want?

This inquiry becomes interesting when you begin to realize who is *the one* that is hidden behind everything you do. What is the very nature of *the doer* within you? Because, naturally, you have a lot to do and are maybe used to saying: *"I have a lot on my plate right now; I don't have time for these kinds of questions."* And then, you go on doing what you always do, meaning, *you just do*.

Now, imagine having a clear overview of the reason for everything you do. In other words, what if you could target the very goal of your life and stick to it until its perfect accomplishment in order to enjoy the fruits of all your actions; would that not be interesting? Rather than just doing what you do, you would do it with a clear vision of what you're seeking through your actions and thus you would immediately be more efficient. You would stop wasting time, and rather than having a more or less boring life, you would carry a constant passion for the real goal of your life.

Through everything you do, without paying attention to it, you are in fact looking for yourself. You are looking for "a you" who would be fulfilled, "a you" who would lack nothing, "a you" who would be fully happy with nothing more *to do* to gain this happiness. No matter what you do, it is to reach the point where you no longer have to do it. You often say: *"when it's done, it's done"* and then you are at peace because, rather than doing, you can now BE, and being is to be happy.

You can reverse this excess of doing by consciously stopping your actions for a short time to feel your own presence and enter into a natural inner state of being. In Yoga Practice, this is called "**Meditation on the Self.**" Anyone can do it, and when you catch yourself in a state of extreme agitation and stress because you have so much to do, remember that you are stressed because you have lost touch with yourself. Breathe deeply, become aware of your inner state of agitation, calm down and repeat: *"I am not what I am doing. I am the quiet witness of what I am doing. My inner being is now at peace with what I have to do. I come back to myself and remove all the stress accumulated in my endeavors. Now, I can constantly act quietly with a feeling of security. In what I am doing, what is most important is the inner state in which I am. I can do anything and be relaxed."*

By being aware of your own presence, your own being, while you are doing what you have to do, you will, without a doubt, increase your efficiency, your harmony, your happiness and the happiness of everyone around you. You will be a pleasant person for everyone you meet.

May each of you remember to take some time to BE, to enjoy the simplicity of life and the harmony residing in every moment.

ACTION AND REACTION

Do you act or do you react?

It is very common to think that everything we do in terms of thinking, talking or doing, is the result of a conscious choice. But if you look more closely, you will realize that for most of the things you do, you are in fact compelled to do them. You never decide to think; your mind forces you to do so. You do not choose the words that are going to be said; your mind makes them arise within you. You do not act; you constantly react according to what your mind sees as being acceptable or unacceptable, pleasant or unpleasant, likable or dislikable. You are constantly torn between accepting and rejection. What you accept or deny must fit your own inner world, which is made of your own certainties and truths. It is a small world that can be destroyed at any moment through your interaction with the real world. Each time the reality of the world does not correspond to what you are expecting from your own inner world, then emotions of fear, anger, frustration and stress arise. You may not be ready to accept the reality of each event as it happens, and this is why you experience a life full of conflicts, contradictions and suffering, even while you hope to find happiness in everything that you do.

Happiness bursts out like a spring as soon as you maintain within yourself the importance of accepting what happens as it is, before you deform and color it with the rigidity of your own inner emotional world.

If you do not accept things as they are because of your very personal expectations, then you become the puppet of your emotions and you begin feeling all kinds of frustrations that make you fragile, anxious and fearful. From this place, you do not act appropriately; you just react because you are moved.

If you see and accept things as they are because they are *just happening*, you cannot be moved. From there, you are able to make the right decisions, not according to what you want, but to what can and must be done for the best development of the situation and the benefit of all.

Be careful, one moment at a time; happiness is within your reach if you do not react but act!

Consider any problem as an opportunity

When you have a problem, there is no point in getting irritated and digging your heels in because of it. This attitude is absolutely ineffective. It does not help at all! In the face of painful and undesirable situations, it is extremely important to keep telling yourself that it is useless to characterize them as problems or to be irritated.

Certain situations are manageable, while others must simply be endured. Even though we regret that our house is not made of gold, we have no way to turn bricks into bullions. Even though we are sorry that the earth is not heaven, it is impossible for us to transform earth into heaven, so it is pointless to fret about such things. No matter how we look at a problem or get irritated by the least little thing about someone, it is simply pointless to worry about it.

If you keep in mind the positive aspects of difficult situations, you can make them participate in transforming your thoughts into high wisdom. Instead of being negative, all your problems become valuable, positive and useful.

To perceive the inconveniences caused by animate or inanimate beings as problems has significant disadvantages. Think deeply about the problems that you have already encountered in your life and the result you obtained when you saw them as problems. Then, develop a powerful motivation and make yourself this promise: "*From now on, whatever problems I meet, I will not be irritated by them. I will not think of them as problems, but see them as positive experiences.*" It is very important to courageously acquire this determination.

If, every time you meet unfavorable circumstances, you automatically consider them to be positive in some way, you will be

consistently happy. Even if criticism, poverty, difficulties, failure, illness or even death are poured on you, nothing will disturb
your mind. Naturally and effortlessly, you will be conscious of
the positive aspects of "problems." And the more you see these
benefits, the happier you will be to experience these difficulties
in your life.

By training one's mind, by getting used to not seeing problems as such, the worst mental or physical pain becomes so easy
to bear and is perceived as quite manageable. One values the
problems that one meets, and they become as light and soft as
cotton.

Be peaceful in everything, and all will be well!

Three reasons for not gossiping

My Spiritual Master left me a very interesting Teaching about gossiping and I am sure you will enjoy reading it. This is a story between the great philosopher Socrates and one of his gossiping disciples. In ancient Greece, Socrates was widely lauded for his wisdom.

One day the great philosopher came upon an acquaintance who ran up to him excitedly and said, *"Socrates, do you know what I just heard about one of your students?"*

"Wait a moment", Socrates replied. *"Before you tell me your story, I'd like you to pass a little test. It's called the Test of Three."*

"The test of three?" asked the man.

"That's right", Socrates continued. *"Before you talk to me about my student, let's take a moment to test what you're going to say."*

*"The first is the test of **Truthfulness**. Have you made absolutely sure that what you are about to tell me is true?"*

"No", the man said, *"actually I just heard about it"*.

"All right", said Socrates. *"So you don't really know whether it's true or not"*.

*"Now let's try the second test, the test of **Goodness**: Is what you want to tell me about my student something good?"*

"No, on the contrary..."

"So", Socrates continued, *"you want to tell me something bad about him even though you're not certain it's true?"*

The man shrugged, a little embarrassed.

Socrates continued. *"You may still pass, though, because there is a third test; it's the filter of **Usefulness**. Is what you want to tell me about my student going to be useful to me in light of your other two answers?"*

"No, not really..."

"Well", concluded Socrates, *"if what you want to tell me is neither true nor good nor even useful, why tell it to me at all? I am not interested in gossip."*

Be careful about what you are about to say!

May this teaching bring more and more truthfulness in what we all say!

To act or to react? That is the question.

No matter what situation you encounter in life, you will always have two choices: to act or to react. To react is to be under the influence of your emotions, with a more or less rigid attitude. When you react, you do not solve a situation as it is, but rather you are compulsively pushed to act according to what you *think* about the situation. If your action is only a reaction, then you will never be able to resolve a situation. Actually, your response will often make things even worse.

There are three ways of acting righteously: by thinking, speaking and taking physical action.

If you really want to think, speak or act righteously, you absolutely need to prevent your emotions from falsifying situations. Your emotions, under the form of fear, denial, expectation, and the desire to be obeyed or recognized, constantly poison you and the people around you. But if you truly wish to be balanced and fair for yourself and for others, it is absolutely possible to do something about them.

To rid yourself of the influence of your emotions, you must try to be conscious of what you are comprised of at every moment, especially when you are faced with challenging situations. Ask yourself *what your inner atmosphere is right now. Are you tense, stressed, angry or scared?* If so, then, willingly put yourself in the position of a conscious, kind, logical and pragmatic observer; one who does not want his or her emotions to deform the situation. If you no longer want to be the victim of your emotions, you must maintain your will to resolve any situation not for your own selfish benefit according to your wishes or preferences, but sincerely for the sole benefit of the situation and those around you.

Remove from your heart the expectation of being immediately understood or obeyed. Let people gain in wisdom and awaken within their own lives. In doing so, you will cease to be afflicted by inner conflict or contradiction, as everything will go smoothly in your life, no matter what the conditions. Remember that you can never truly be opposed to what is happening since it is happening. To accept what is *as it is*, is the best attitude to help any situation unfold harmoniously.

This inner attitude will quickly bring about harmonious relationships with everyone around you and with your life as a whole.

May peace, love and harmony accompany you day and night.

Do you make good decisions?

Before you throw yourself into action, ask yourself: "*What do I want to obtain?*" During the action you might think: "Yes, I'm getting exactly what is needed", but after the action ask yourself: "*What did I really get?*"

When you make a decision, you must hold on to it no matter what. But remember that you must decide according to the situation and your abilities, and according to the needs of the situation rather than your needs through the situation. Take everything into consideration, including yourself and your inner attitude regarding the situation. As soon as you have resolved not to change your decision, you will feel strong. While your decision is being accomplished, you could decide to do more or to improve your decision but don't change it, because if you do, if you do not accomplish it, you will lose confidence in yourself.

Don't rush into a decision. If you make a decision but you feel in conflict with the situation, take more time to study the circumstances, even if it means postponing the decision to improve it. A good decision always brings peace, kindness and happiness to you and others. You must also know that, if you are troubled or uncomfortable with your decision, it means that your decision will not bring good fruits. For your decision to be beneficial for you and everyone, be sure that there is as little emotion involved in your decision as possible. Remember that any bad outcome that you could have experienced in the past because of your decisions was only caused by unidentified upsetting emotions, which deformed the necessity of the situation.

To avoid any mistake and to be free to make good decisions, be sure that you are free from personal emotions by being aware of them. When you know something, you become free from it. If you want to make a good decision, be sure that none of your emotions are involved in it and always act according to the necessity of the situation and the happiness of everyone around you.

May all of you make good decisions for everyone to be happy and harmonious around you.

Do you prefer good news or bad news?

Have you ever noticed that most of the time you expect good news rather than bad news and that you prefer good news to bad news?

The reason for your preference of good news lies in the effect certain news has on you due to the accumulation of emotions already residing within you. You prefer good news because they give rise to happy and joyous feelings. For this reason, you constantly hope for good news. You also constantly hope you don't receive bad news as it generates tumultuous and disagreeable feelings such as disappointment, frustration, fear, hatred, anxiety, doubt, and the like.

If you reflect on this, you will easily conclude that no matter what kind of news you receive, it never carries *in itself* any agreeable or disagreeable emotions. Therefore, good news or bad news cannot exist. It is a question of logic. News is never responsible for any emotional reactions. It is rather one's emotions that create a positive or negative reaction to the news.

Once you understand this, it is important to observe yourself when you receive any kind of news, whether written or verbal. Realize that although you cannot choose the kind of news you receive, you always have a choice regarding your reaction to it.

In yoga we call this practice, "the control of emotions" (*Samskarakshaya in Sanskrit*). This practice is essential, because if you don't control your emotions, they will control and overwhelm you against your will.

Trying to act under the influence of an emotion is as dangerous as drunk driving. The result is often catastrophic because through an emotion, you react rather than act.

Whatever the news, it is just news. Don't blame the news when it is the fault of your emotions. There is nothing more powerful in destroying the effect of an emotion (especially a negative one) than to see it, perceive it, and be aware of its presence. As soon as you are aware of an emotion in you, the emotion loses its power over your consciousness.

When you receive news, remember to tell yourself that it is just news and that it should be taken quietly, with neutrality and equanimity. The news should always be accepted for what it is first so that you're able to respond as you must and not as you want. Choose what is right over what you prefer and you will always be at peace with life.

There is no good news or no bad news! There is just news! Protect peace, lucidity and joy by being vigilant with regard to your emotions!

Respecting the law of the unexpected

Have you ever noticed that no matter what you plan, it never materializes exactly as you imagined? For example, you plan to leave for the grocery store and return home at a certain time, but for one reason or another, you are not back when you expected. Sometimes you expect people to act in a certain way and, strangely, they act in opposition to your expectation. Though it may seem easy to make things happen as you wish, no matter what you plan, the forces in action always seem to challenge those plans and expectations. When everything goes as you expect, you think it's normal, but when things don't fit your expectations, you find it frustrating. The reality is that your plans are often thwarted rather than obeyed by daily circumstances. The reason why so many people get frustrated with life is because they try to plan everything in their minds, but do not take into consideration that their own inner world doesn't correspond to the real world. In the real world, there are tremendous forces at play, which can thwart what people wish, expect or plan for.

Since there are more things that you don't know than things that you do know, plan what you want, but always be ready for the unexpected. Remember that nothing in the totality of creation is static and even more importantly, nothing revolves around you and your plans. This is especially true for people, since people are in constant flux due to their lack of control over their emotions. In less than five minutes, your best friend or relative can have a change of mood and suddenly not be as open to you and your expectation as you'd hoped. The lack of respect of the *law of the unexpected* in daily life is the cause of so much misunderstanding and rancor between people and nations.

In yoga practice, working with the unexpected is called *"becoming lucid and adaptable."*

To be *lucid* is to remember that due to the numerous forces in action at any given time in the world, there is a big difference between what one wants and what actually happens. For example, you may crave chocolate, but it just so happens that there is none left in the cupboard to satiate your craving.

To be *adaptable* is to remember that you must accept *all* situations, as they could not be otherwise, and from this acceptance, you can take the wisest possible action. For example, you may despise that someone spoke harshly to you, but they did, and being upset is not going to change that. In any circumstance, it is always better to tell yourself that what happened cannot be changed and that you must act according to the reality of it rather than to what you wanted or expected. Do not oppose what is to what you think should be; be one with what is so that you can act efficiently.

Respect the law of the unexpected with lucidity and adaptability, and you will experience a constant increase of happiness and joy in your heart. Try following this advice and you will be amazed by its power to invoke freedom in your life!

How to definitively solve a difficult situation

As you experience it, life is an endless series of unexpected situations. You can plan anything you want, but it never turns out as you wish, as there is always a little something that happens beyond your expectation and control.

Maybe this is the case for you right now and you're facing an *adverse situation*, meaning a situation that goes against all your expectations. Perhaps you are disagreeing with a family member or friend, or are experiencing frustrations arising from conflict with those you care about. Maybe something in your daily life isn't turning out as you hoped or you're experiencing a period of your life where you feel depressed about your circumstances and relationships. All kinds of events can make you feel that you are facing a *difficult situation*, especially when you don't have a proper solution in sight. If this is happening to you, there are four things you must consider.

- First of all, you should know that there are no difficult situations in life but only situations that unfold according to actions that took place in the past. We call this *the natural course of events*. So, no matter what position you are in right now, stop calling it "difficult" as sooner or later, every situation finds its own solution according to the different elements that compose and interact with the situation.

- Secondly, either you can change, improve, and harmonize the situation right now or you can't because the situation does not fulfill all the necessary conditions for it to be solved. If you can harmonize or solve the situation in any way at this moment through a specific action, then do it. If you cannot change it at this time, then don't do anything. Just breathe deeply, relax and keep a positive attitude knowing that this situation is bound to eventually find a harmonious solution.

- Thirdly, notice how your frustration within the situation makes you perceive it as more dramatic than it is. Frustration is always based upon an egoistic and selfish point of view. If this is the case for you and you are vexed, shocked, frustrated or angry, then remind yourself that you lack objectivity on the situation as you are deforming it through the prism of your emotions. Calm down, recognize the negative effect of your emotions upon the situation, then resolve to apprehend it and solve it with a genuinely objective and correct attitude. Remember that you don't want to get hurt and no one else wants to get hurt either.

- Fourthly, do not react, but always act according to the necessity of the situation and the happiness of the people related to it. Solve the situation not for your own good but for the good of the situation itself. There is what can be done and what cannot. If you can do it, *do*. If you cannot, *don't*.

May this yogic advice given to me by my own Master be of powerful help in overcoming adversity in your daily life as it did for me.

How to always make a good decision

No matter what life situation you are in, it is obvious that, one way or another, you put yourself into it. Everything you have thought, said or done in the past has led you to exactly where you are now in time and space. There's no need to argue against this! You may like or dislike your position in life right now, but everything that enters in contact with you is in fact telling you something about yourself. Pause, observe attentively, and you will learn so much!

You should consider your life as a chess game, where every move is the carrier of what you will soon experience. So, what will be your next move to achieve your next goal? Are you game enough to become an Awakened Life Player? There are many paths leading to the top of a mountain. You should choose your next move, your next decision in life, with great care. There is always the short path, the long path and the only Right Path, the Perfectly Right Decision to make. If you want to achieve perfection in life, you should consider that the multiple-choice option does not exist; there is only the perfect choice to be made.

For any decision you want to make, whether it is important or without consequence, you must be ready to accept its outcome. Making the perfect decision at every moment of one's life is one of the most captivating practices in Yoga Sadhana because it demands a great deal of observation, clarity of mind and awareness of one's own inner atmosphere. If you are not calm and pragmatic enough, or if you are under the influence of an emotional eruption, then you can be sure that no matter what kind of decision you make, it will be a disaster.

First of all, to make a good decision, you need to observe the facts beyond your preferences. It's not about what you would like to be or obtain anymore; it is: *what are the facts*? Stick to the facts! If it is to choose a new job or to solve a complex relationship problem with someone, try to see the facts as they are. Write down a precise description of the elements that concern you and how you feel about the situation at this moment; try to be as neutral as possible. To make a good decision, you need to *aspire* to make the good decision. Keep this noble aspiration in mind while observing the pure facts and surrender the situation.

Secondly, treat any decision you have to make as if you were advising your best friend. A personal decision must be treated as if it concerned someone else. The first thing you would say to your best friend would be to calm down, to breathe and to remove all sensations of feeling rushed. Refuse to make any decision based on an explosion of emotion. An emotion, no matter its nature, tends to deform the facts. Get rid of the dangerous habit of dramatizing *what is*. What is should be accepted *as it is* and then improved through a rational decision.

Thirdly, reflect upon what result you expect from the decision you have to make. A good decision should bring you immediate peace and make you and all of the people involved very happy. No matter what kind of decision you have to make, it should always be because you want to be happier and make others happier.

There are decisions that concern only you, and others that involve other people's lives. If you are talking about eating cookies, for example, it concerns mostly you. But if you are talking about getting married or divorced, then it concerns your partner and your family, and this is where the art of gathering the right conditions to make a good decision is capital.

The more you seek to make a harmonious decision for the benefit of as many people as possible and the more you cease seeking only for your own satisfaction, the more you will experience that making a choice, even in the most adverse situation, can bring you a feeling of freedom and fulfillment.

If it is easy to make small, inconsequential decisions, you can be sure that life will soon put you in delicate situations where you will have to excel in the Art of Deciding Wisely.

No matter what kind of big or small decision you have to make, remember that nothing lasts forever and that 10 years from now, your problem will be resolved and you will have to live with the consequence of your present choices.

The best indication of a perfect decision is that it always brings you a feeling of Liberation, Love, and Harmony as soon as you know what to do without any doubt.

I hope that this Yogic Advice given to me by my own spiritual Master, His Holiness the Lord Hamsah Manarah, will be useful in your own life.

THE MIND

The Treasury of your thoughts

A very important method to discovering spiritual Energy is through the development of positive thoughts. This can be done by increasing the profoundness of your thoughts and the realization of their impact around you. Every human being is the result of his or her way of thinking. Apart from the Supreme Self within you, you are nothing but an illusory manifestation, created by the magic of your thoughts. All your life circumstances are only the result of your thought forces.

How can you maintain a higher level of thinking at all times? Is it by harboring positive thoughts and eliminating negative thoughts? How can you sustain spiritual power in a world where insecurity prevails; where so many things distract and unbalance the mind, albeit through grief or pleasure, gain or loss?

Every human being is linked to the cosmic process of thoughts, and thus attracts forces from the akashic subtle plane (*ethereal plane*) where thoughts move about. If your mind emits low vibrations and is negatively oriented, you crystallize karmic forces (*suffering*) in the cosmos. If, for example, you slip into depression and when you are in this state you connect with people who are demoralized, you will find that your own negative thoughts become reinforced, which leads to an even greater disturbance.

Similarly, if your mind is in a positive state, you will draw positive thought schemes to yourself. When you meet people who act this way, you are bound to notice how powerfully they function with these subtle and magical elements that fill their atmosphere. These people are actually supported by the Shakti (Universal Force) that has accumulated around them, day after day, because they act consciously by controlling their mind and always directing it toward the positive.

Knowing this secret, you must be vigilant and be really interested in discovering your true nature. The integral yoga that we practice at the Ashram is a process brought on by an intense interest in discovering one's true Self. Knowing that your thoughts are your treasure, you must not waste them. On the contrary, you must become capable of identifying and multiplying this treasure of your thoughts.

You must keep alive within yourself a vigilant understanding, and not allow any negative thoughts to arise in you. Also observe your actions, as what you do and think can tint your mind and drag it down or up.

Be positive, even and especially in adversity! Nothing lasts, everything changes, everything transforms itself. An outcome favorable to your evolution will emerge through your positive connection with the Divine Force, which sustains the entire creation.

May Peace be always in your mind!

Does your mind generate truly good intentions?

Whatever the task we are engaged in, whether it is ordinary or mundane, related to our spiritual practice or not, our intention is fundamental.

Why? Because our mind plays a major role in everything; it is all-powerful. What creates the good in this world is the mind; what creates the bad is also the mind. And this is also true for peace and happiness in this world. Whether it is happiness or suffering, it does not come from the outside, but from our own mind.

In the same way, what determines our actions to be harmonious or fair comes from inside of us. It is called our *motivation*. Motivation is the intention we carry within.

If we mix our intention with negative emotions such as jealousy, anger, fear or suspicion, then our immensely powerful mind will create unhappy conditions in our life and that of others.

We must constantly discriminate between our good and bad intentions. If our intention is bad, that is, selfish or filled with negative emotions, we must do our best to completely transform it by removing negative or selfish elements from it. We must always sincerely participate in the happiness of all sentient beings around us.

This is the key to spreading happiness in the hearts of those we love and everyone in the world.

Do you *use your mind* or are you *used by your mind?*

Have you ever taken a moment to observe what is going on in your head or to stop and ponder why you think what you are thinking about right now? Do you make the decision to think or are you compelled to think in your own unique way? If you pay even the slightest attention to what is going on in your head, you will quickly realize that no matter what you think about, it is always somehow imposed upon you. You may believe that you think freely according to your own will, but have you ever tried to not think at all? What would you experience if you weren't having all these thoughts arising, one after another, in your head throughout the day?

This is the very reason why we are so interested in practicing Meditation at the Ashram. The experiences of great Yogi Masters throughout millennia have proven that beyond the thought process, there is another level of existence that is called *Pure Consciousness* or a *Pure State of Being*.

In your mind, the *you* that you are is the result of all the past memories that you've acquired since birth and even from other lives. In the mind, what are you? Nothing more than your physical body, your personal and partial memories, and an image of yourself, a mere reflection of yourself which you call *me*, meaning your personality, your ego; that's it! But beyond your mind, the true *you* is not your physical body, nor your memories or your ego as a personality, but it is Pure Freedom, a pure Consciousness freed from all limitations regarding time, space and causality, which is called your *Essential Presence* or the *Central Being*, called the *Atman* in the Sanskrit Sacred Scriptures.

If you observe what is going on in your head, it is easy to verify that you don't think freely as you are always the unconscious follower of thoughts that arise without having been invited or consciously "ordered" by you. One of the most important observations in yoga is to realize that you don't use your mind but you are used by it. All the thoughts that rise in your conscious mind have been triggered by emotions and impressions coming from your past. You think the way you think mostly because you want to protect yourself from the possible return of painful experiences that you've had in the past. No matter what you think of, even the slightest thought, it is always because of your past, not because of the present. Since everything that is thought in your head is based upon past impressions, can you be sure that what you are thinking about right now corresponds to the reality of the present moment? Knowing that every moment is absolutely unique and has never happened before, how do you intend to respond perfectly to the present situation if everything going on in your head stems from the past? In simpler terms, how do you evaluate your present situation? Is it based upon the past, or can you go beyond the mind by eliminating the past and seeing the world as it really is for the first time?

These are very interesting questions for which the answer can become an inner experience discovered through a more and more extensive observation of your mind, not as a "victim" of your thoughts and emotions but as an increasingly quiet and vigilant Witness of your own way of thinking in your own world. In doing so, you will soon experience the Reality of the Real World which, by the way, has nothing to do with the way you have thought the world until now.

May all this logical and pragmatic reflection make you eager to *use your mind* rather than be *used by it*. Be careful, the mind is tricky; it is the master of all illusions! My beloved Guru used to say: "*Don't believe everything that pops up in your head!*" and He was so right!

FEAR

Why are you afraid?

All emotions are based on fear: fear of the unknown, fear of being hungry or thirsty, of being hot or cold, fear of losing loved ones or friends, losing one's social position or one's financial security, not to mention the deep-rooted fear of illness, old age and death.

The fear originating from desire is one of being separated from what is pleasant. With aversion, it is the fear of meeting what is unpleasant. With jealousy, it is the fear of being outmatched by others or of not being able to fulfill one's objectives. With pride, it is the fear of being criticized or not being recognized by others. With ignorance, it is the dread of change and denial of the impermanence of all phenomena.

The great goal of life is the awakened state of your consciousness!

It is a process of opening, similar to that of a flower blooming in the spring. At first, because of doubts, we are somewhat closed, like a bud. Then, gradually, we dare to open ourselves to the light of wisdom, love and compassion, as well as to all the qualities that exist as potential in every one of us.

The moment fear stops is when we begin to experiment with the essential nature of our own presence. The whole dualistic attitude and all the conflicted emotions are released in this total opening of the mind. There is no longer someone within who always wants to control everything and who fights to be victorious over the world.

This is the understanding that there is nothing left to defend and that all of our fears are the result of our self-image, which has absolutely no reality at the ultimate level of our presence and our consciousness.

To exit our mental story and the character we believe ourselves to be playing and, to return to the true present of one's presence while accepting whatever happens in order to better face it, allows for everyone to discover that fear is only a mental reflex created to protect the ego, having no roots in the true reality.

No longer be afraid!

Fear is the most stressful emotion because it paralyzes objectivity and clarity of mind, and makes you see reality as distorted. Fear makes you focus on what you do not want to happen and what you judge to be unacceptable in your life. Most people spend their entire lives fighting against what they deem to be "the worst", that which they think will prevent them from being completely happy. In an ordinary mind, fear is dominant and it unconsciously controls all of one's actions, even the action of thinking.

When you realize this, you understand that no matter what kind of fear is within you, it occurs because you are denying, rejecting or not accepting what is as it is. You also realize that the conflict created by fear is never related to the situation, but only to you. In the practice of Yoga in daily life, I teach aspirants to deal with fear by realizing that no matter what they want or do not want, like or dislike, that right now, what is happening *is happening*, and that nothing can ever change the nature of a situation that has already occurred.

It is erroneous to think that it's possible to deny a situation since, in every circumstance, the situation is *as it is*, and it cannot be otherwise for the time being. By being aware of your own fear while you integrate a situation, you will easily see that you cannot make a good decision until you have first fully accepted the situation *as it is*. To do so, learn to say "Yes" to what is before taking any action so that you can respond to the necessity of the situation rather than wanting the situation to be different or as you would like it to be. At any moment, nothing can be different from what it is. Accept this once and for all and free yourself from all conflicts.

Take your fear into consideration in all situations, then accept the situation *as it is* to quiet your mind so you can act properly, rather than reacting inappropriately through a denial of the situation.

From there, you will discover that fear was your only true enemy and that you can overcome it easily by accepting more and denying less. To act correctly, stop reacting and be free from fear.

May all good things be granted to you as you face all situations, good and bad, in a balanced manner!

What are you worried about?

No matter what kind of challenge you are facing right now, there is no justification for being worried about it. Worrying is nothing more than a habit of dramatizing what should not be a drama but a simple fact. You can easily realize that you are never actually worried about a situation; rather you are worried about the imagined outcome of it. The situation is *as it is* and if you are worried about anything, it is always about the imagined impact of the situation. When you are stressed, worried or anxious, it is not because of any kind of situation; it is always because of something that you fear within the situation. The situation does not carry your fear; you carry it yourself.

To easily overcome any worries or stress, it is important to ask to yourself: *"What am I afraid of about this situation?"* From here, you will realize that what you are afraid of is not determined by you, but by the natural unfolding of the situation. You cannot control a situation; you can only take control of yourself to improve what follows a situation. When you understand that you cannot change a situation that is happening or has happened, especially by being worried about it, then you understand that the only good thing to do is to be at peace with it no matter what. No situation ever belongs to you, so don't make it yours, even if it concerns things that belong to you or people with whom you are in relation with. Things and people, even people dear to you, don't belong to you; you are merely in contact with them. In daily Yoga Practice, we call this *"to depersonalize a situation"* or to not make it personal.

By doing so, you will keep from being in conflict with any situation that doesn't need to be altered but instead needs to be appreciated as it is; not as you would like it to be. From there, you will become the witness of your emotions and in the process of analyzing the situation; you will quickly learn the difference between the situation and your emotions. An immediate peace and a feeling of inner security will overwhelm your state of mind with a deep sentiment that, in reality, everything is constantly as it must be. The proof of it is that nothing is ever different from what it is.

I hope these elements will help you to face the adversity of your emotions with a great deal of courage and wisdom. Don't worry, nothing lasts forever, the sun will soon shine again!

Do not get tense, worried or anxious.
It doesn't help!

No matter what is happening to you or what you think is going to happen to you, you will never get out of it with tension, worry or anxiety. Try to remain aware of the danger of your tendency of seeing the glass as half empty. The human mind originates from the animal kingdom where you can easily be eaten by something bigger than you. For your mind, the worst outcome is always lurking around the corner. So, it is an instrument essentially made to detect what can harm or destroy you. You should sincerely contemplate how you let your mind use you rather than being the one using it!

In the practice of Yoga, our Guru (*Spiritual Teacher*) quickly teaches us how important it is to differentiate between one's mind and one's consciousness. The mind contains all the memories and impressions you have recorded since birth and also those from previous lives. All these impressions are still alive within you in the forms of emotion and desire. Out of these arises what you want to get or to do and what you *don't* want to get or to do!

It is more or less through these unconscious memories that you tend to react rather than act. Your mind solely works through an automatic process of comparison, confusing *what is* with *what was*. It superimposes impressions coming from the past upon the reality of what is. Then, as a result, you no longer receive *news*, rather you receive *good* or *bad* news; a situation does not simply happen, it happens with the added qualification of good or bad, favorable or unfavorable. But *according to what*? According to what you like or dislike, what you want or don't want. This all takes place without realizing that no matter what you prefer, things just happen; situations only unfold according to previous causes and it cannot be otherwise.

So, accept what is *as it is first*. Then, put forth the effort to not want something different, since what has happened cannot be changed anyhow. From there, try to see if you can improve the situation within the context of this very moment or if it needs more time and a deeper level of reflection before you can move forward. No matter what, you should always remain at peace with *what is*. If this is too difficult due to the influence of your emotions, then do not act; take a deep breath, quiet down, don't talk, don't make any decisions, and wait until your inner atmosphere is clear. A good decision is always accompanied by a peaceful and balanced mind originating from a non-egoistic point of view of the situation.

I hope these vastly proven recommendations from Yogic Practice will help you obtain a happier life and a better outcome in harmonizing unexpected situations.

With Love and Blessing to all of you on the Path of Life.

Overcoming discouragement and depression

In life, it is possible to experience moments of discouragement and depression, where a feeling of past failure is added to your analysis of the situation at hand, forcing you to adhere to a more or less dark vision of your life. This can easily be overcome and, if you are going through such a period laden with obstacles and frustrations, it is capital for you to be extremely careful regarding the dark power of the mind, which can make you see yourself as darker than you are in reality.

There are a few rules you must constantly remember if you want to go beyond the spells of discouragement and depression:

1. First of all, nothing is wrong in your life since things only happen. From now on, break the habit of dealing with problems; only deal with what happens without qualifying anything as good or bad.

2. Second, no matter what happens in your life, it always corresponds to you: it is you who is in this situation right now. Therefore, you are certainly the best and most qualified person to deal with it harmoniously and successfully.

3. Third, you cannot and should never disagree with what happens, since what is happening can absolutely not be otherwise at this moment of your life. Accept that what is is *as it is* and remain calm.

4. Fourth, nothing lasts forever, meaning that adversity in life always has an end. After the rain, sooner or later, the sun shines again; you can count on this! What seems harsh today will vanish on the time line; you can be sure of it! Trust that impermanence will bring you good fortune along the Path of Life and don't be burdened by the unfoldment of your incarnation!

You should realize that any feeling of discouragement or depression is in fact a powerful call for happiness and freedom. Focus on the fact that you don't want to be discouraged or depressed, rather that you wish to be happy; this should be absolutely clear in your mind and be your primary motivation. Assert: "*I don't want to be discouraged or depressed, I just want to be happy and this is my goal no matter what!*"

If you want to be happy no matter what you are going through, you must stop fighting against reality. Reality is as it is right now and you can't do anything about it. If you accept reality *as it is*, you will immediately stop fighting against it. From there, you will easily see what can and must be done now or later. For example, before you are able to repair your car, you first need to accept that your car is broken. First admit, *My car is broken*, and then declare, *Now I can and must repair it or get a new one*. Another example could be that of leaving your husband or wife. In such circumstances, you should first accept that s/he is *as s/he is* right now, since they cannot be otherwise. Acceptance brings you peace of mind and clarity for all future decisions. Accept first, don't blame anyone or anything, breathe deeply, and once you are quiet enough, apply the right solution for the happiness and benefit of as many people as possible. In reality, you are never stuck anywhere or with anyone. There is always a solution!

These are the most important rules of a Yoga Sadhana Practice in your daily life. In following this advice, the words "discouragement" and "depression" will soon have no meaning for you!

May these powerful keys given to me by my Guru when I was very young help you achieve an ever-heightened level of harmony and happiness with everyone.

To Cure Oneself of Fear

All emotions are based in fear: fear of the unknown, fear of being hungry or thirsty, hot or cold, fear we might lose our loved ones or friends, fear of losing our social position or material security, as well as the deep-rooted fear of illness, old age and death. Our situation in the world is often challenging because happiness escapes us and suffering hounds us. To get out of this rut is to discover something new, yet we must have the courage to go beyond our fears and to develop enough confidence to move toward the unknown.

Sometimes, the walls of our prison must close in on us, nearly choking us, before we become willing to seek a way out. When suffering becomes unbearable, confidence in ourselves and in others is the key that will unlock the door of our prison. Confidence allows us to let go of what is known in order to move toward the unknown; to abandon our bad habits, to turn toward what is beneficial, and to transform our negative vision of existence into a positive one. Only then can we take the risk of leaving all that is limited and familiar in order to discover a new perspective on life.

The instant fear ceases to rule us is when we can begin exploring the essential nature of our consciousness, which, although it observes our fear, is not itself this fear. Fear is a present moment projection of the worst possible outcomes that could happen on the timeline of our lives. It is unreal and unjustified. Remain with the facts without deforming them and greet every situation as it is. This will always give your consciousness the peace that makes it lucid and efficient and is sure to bring about happiness for everyone.

Your consciousness is never the object or the subject of fear; its nature is free and strong, and in it, you are always outside the reach of forces that will try to thwart you. Fear nothing and face everything with a balanced vision, one moment at a time. Know that any adverse situation will pass like the clouds in the blue sky of your presence, your Consciousness that is the witness.

PAST, PRESENT AND FUTURE

Is the tiger of the past pursuing you?

Don't look back, there is a tiger behind you, and it's no ordinary tiger... it's an illusory monster!

First: Do not let your mind fall into nostalgia through fascination with past memories. Understand that the past was not as delightful as you imagine it was. Also, do not spend time blaming the past for the present circumstances.

Second: Do not let your mental space empty itself of consciousness; keep it involved in actions that are beneficial to your evolution, actions that your mind will not have time to drown under illusory thoughts. Use all of your talents to do good unto others. Your future depends on what you do right now, so do it with perseverance and consciousness. If you act rightly today, you are preparing an excellent future for yourself and also for others.

Third: When you think about the past, you are actually thinking about only one aspect of it. It's an incomplete memory. From a distance, things often appear wonderful, as distance is a source of illusions.

That is why we started by saying *not to look back, that there is a tiger behind you, and it's not an ordinary tiger, but an illusory monster!*

When you understand this correctly, and you can look back

and see that not only has the monster disappeared, but the past itself has disappeared, then... all you will see is the Light of your own Self projected limitlessly for the happiness of all beings.

Accepting change

Because of the natural irritation that change usually provokes in us, we have a tendency to build our world on the pretense that we harbor stability and security. But if we take a closer look, we will see that we can never escape change. We can take out an insurance policy against old age, illness, or death, but it is only a contract with time, not with the truth! The same applies to our sense of self. Clinging to our personality is our insurance against "bruises to our ego", but again, it is only a contract with time, not with the truth. Truth is beyond time, and beyond a self that would be separate from the Whole. Rather than running around searching for the fake stability and security of the ego, we must learn to remain quiet and see clearly the truth of the change that is necessary for our evolution. Through every change, the Divine gives us the opportunity to see what is experiencing change within us.

This is the ultimate Self-seeking Itself in the Absolute!

The past has disappeared,
and the future does not (and never will) exist.
What is left to us?

Have you ever contemplated the extent to which *what you do* is based upon a degree of happiness that you hope to appreciate at a more or less future time. No matter what you do, it is to be happier later, either at the time you carry it out or once it's complete. The human mind works along a timeline comprised only of past and future. The present is rarely experienced because it is the only reality the ordinary mental human being doesn't live in. Your reality as a "thinking being" is only made of conjectures about the past or a more or less promising future. No matter what kind of future you project ahead of you, it is a pure invention and you will never reach it because the future never happens. No one ever goes into the future; that's a fact! You can only be in the present. Have you ever travelled into the future since you were born? No! Then, why do you constantly project yourself there?

For an awakened human being, the past and the future are total nonsense. To think about something is only to reflect about a mirage, an inconsistent, immaterial and unreal subject, object or idea. You only carry the illusion of coming from the past and moving toward the future when in reality the only thing you have, or will ever experience in your life, is the present. The present is not something that is going to happen in two seconds or in a minute. No, the present is only *you*, right here, right now in this very tiny instant while you are reading this part of the article. It is only in the here and now that you can be aware of yourself reading this article, not later today or tomorrow. Yesterday is an elusive memory and tomorrow is a subjective projection of your mind on a timeline that doesn't actually contain past or future, but only the present moment. At every moment, there is only the reality of the instant; there is no difference between eternity and the present moment.

These elements about the nature of time are among the most important to learn along the Path leading to Self-Discovery. Thinking about yourself or others in the past or the future is not a problem as long as you remember that you have never been and *never will be* in the past or the future because you can only be in the present. This is why in Yoga, the practice of meditation is so important; because we realize that if we want to discover the Secret of Life, the very Nature of our own Self, it can only be experienced through a serious practice where we sit and keep our mind where it belongs: here and now. Through this practice, you enter into another dimension, a timeless dimension, a dimension in which time is no longer important; an amazing dimension in which only your presence is important. Here and now, it is easy to experience that all fears we carry within ourselves, all suffering we secretly bear, are only fixed in our ideas about the past and our anticipation of the future. If you realize that there is truly no past or future and you come back to exactly where you are – here and now – then you realize that fear and suffering are no longer a part of your reality.

Here and now is the only safe place in life because as soon as you start remembering your past or experiencing anxiety about the future, you start reacting like a "dream walker" who believes that what the mind produces is real. Wake up and come back to the reality of here and now, where there is only the present moment, and in this very moment there is just what happens; not what *has* happened, what *will* happen, or what you think is going to happen. No matter how you think about your future, it is never going to happen the way you think. I know many people, for example, who are afraid of dying. It sometimes becomes an obsession for them, and they don't realize that the way they are going to die has nothing to do with what they imagine. They should come back to the present moment and stick to it in order to enjoy a real life in which they will cease to be victims of their own mind's deformations. Our only real enemy is our unfortunate identification to the productions of the mind.

Here and now is the only way to experience happiness and oneness in real life. Always come back to the present moment. Don't dramatize, don't let your mind carry you away from the reality of the instant, and I promise you that peace will grow in your heart no matter what.

Getting old is a privilege, not a disadvantage

Nowadays, we live in a world where it is important to be pre-occupied with death. This is indicated by the excess emphasis placed on the eternal youth of this "new god" called *the physical body*. Staying young at all costs for as long as possible and denying the value of old age has become the new dream of our childish humanity.

All the activities for seniors are inspired by the profound conviction that it is horrible to get old and that they must reduce what is hideous in aging. For that reason, old people tend to do things normally accomplished by younger people. If seniors can have a sexual life or can travel around the world, this makes them feel *as though they were still young*, when in fact they *are old*. All these activities that make old people deny the aging process should have been fully experienced at 20, 30 or 40 years old. But as accomplished older beings who have fully realized their human potential, it would be better that they now prepare themselves for *the third age*. An older accomplished Human Being who has reached the third age should learn to progressively detach from the manifested world that he or she will inevitably leave. It is even more important for this older man or woman to discover a profound inner life, a true life of *Being* rather than *having*; a life far richer with the deep meaning of the Essential.

Things are not understood this way nowadays, as aging is misunderstood! People are only interested in old age to try to allow seniors to act as if they were still young. That is not aging; aging is accepting the "change". It is accepting that a page has been turned and that another one is presenting itself. It is also accepting that death completes a chapter of our evolution and begins a new one. One should not be afraid of death, as death is an aspect of life; but most Westerners have forgotten this. To oppose death to life is a mistake, as death is opposed to birth. Life is a constant game of death and birth at every moment. At every moment the past is dead, the entire creation is totally renewed, and nothing remains the same. There is, at every moment and everywhere, a "death-birth process" at all levels of life. Two major events happen to a human being: birth and death. *Birth of what?* Birth of the physical body. *Death of what?* Death of the physical body. But the physical body is not the only reality of a human being. There is the physical reality, there is the "psychic reality" or reality of the subtle bodies of the soul, and there is the spiritual reality of the Self, the Atman or Pure Consciousness.

From there, *what was born?* The physical body. *What is going to die?* The physical body. But beyond the physical body, there is also the soul and the consciousness. A true, entirely manifested human being is the harmonization of the soul and the physical body, sustained by this immutable Consciousness, which is non-affected, universal and beyond the personality.

If you can accept these capital elements of Universal Wisdom, then peace, security and confidence should be with you. No fear of time, no fear of aging; it is the beginning of Eternity. You do not need to reach old age filled with frustration, regrets of your youth, dependence on esthetic surgery and Botox, or obsessive consumption of purely organic food, and so on. No matter what you do, your body will die of old age. Accepting aging is accepting the true Contract of Life, which is that *Everything that is born must die to be born again.*

To discover what is immortal within you, you need to first accept what is mortal within you. And what is mortal is only your body of flesh, your physical body. Getting older and then getting old is an immense privilege, a chance, a Divine Opportunity to enter into a new wise phase of life, a phase where you prepare to let go of what you are not and discover *what you are* beyond this physical body.

May this precious Teaching for Yogis, which was given to me by my Revered Master H. H. the Lord Hamsah Manarah, help those who have difficulty dealing with aging. A page has been turned and another one is now in sight; a new chapter of your Spiritual Evolution must now be prepared.

With love and all my encouragement to those who will face old age with joy and aspiration for the Divine.

THE MEANING OF LIFE

The preciousness of your time in life

In the West, we never have time because we waste it.

People have very little time, especially for spiritual practice, but they have plenty of time for other things that are important to them. We are very busy; our life is often wasted in bustling activity. We wander through the days without a meaningful goal in mind; we waste our time.

We dissipate so much of life; we simply waste time without ever realizing it. We waste time thinking as an ego, wandering about without consciously keeping within the Ultimate Goal of life. We constantly worry about the past, the future, and also the present, without ever really living in the present.

When a very great master, Gyawal Rinpoche, Tibet's 16th Karmapa, was asked what he had noticed about Westerners, answered that: *"They waste time."* But he continued, *"How do they end up wasting time? They are so busy! In fact, it is in their very way of being busy that they waste time."*

So, we must realize how we waste the time of our incarnation by remaining in the unreal world of our thoughts and worries. When it comes to the essential things that concern our Soul, we have little time because we want everything immediately and we tell ourselves that later, we'll have time to seek the essential.

Yet, behind our thoughts, words and actions on the timeline, there is our true consciousness, our true presence. Ask what your pure consciousness would want or do if the demands of your personality allowed consciousness to be itself for but a moment in this life.

To discover that which we truly aspire for beyond all our preoccupations, we must walk the path of inner awakening. This is the time when all our motivations will become evident. We have sought outside for the happiness that we could not find within, but once we find it within, we can offer it to everyone around us, without ever depleting it in ourselves.

Such is the nature of the great goal of this life.

May your lifetime contain billions of moments filled with the happiness that inhabits you.

You are what you are looking for

When you realize that everything you do, beneath all your apparent rationale, is motivated by the search for happiness; you come to realize that you must concentrate all your attention on the properties of this happiness you seek.

When you look for happiness, you are looking to become something. When you become this thing that we call happiness, then you declare, "*I AM happy.*" You do not say: "*I am here, and the happiness is somewhere else.*" The pleasure in happiness comes from your total identification with happiness.

Progressively, you come to know that this happiness is a part of you and that the pleasure you experience in happiness is BEING happiness. You may have thought that you wanted to be close to happiness, but now you realize that you can be close to happiness and remain unhappy! Someone very happy can be right beside you, yet you may still be unhappy.

Happiness, which is called Ananda in Sanskrit, or *Felicity* in yoga, is in fact something that you must become in order to experience it and to be able to say, "*Yes, now I am happy.*" So it is something that flows into and through you and that you then project everywhere.

Why is this so important? Because if you fail to understand that you are the one who projects happiness out of yourself onto any little thing that you like in daily life, you will never realize that **you are the source of this happiness.**

May you keep happiness alive within yourself in all daily situations that you encounter.

Have you done what you had to do in this life?

No matter how old you are, sooner or later we all feel the pressure of the time we have left to live, like a constant reminder of all that remains to be accomplished. Sometimes, it is a vague feeling of having missed the realization of something essential, something that has been hidden, forgotten, or ambiguous in our head. As time passes, the question of the true purpose of existence becomes heavier in the background of your consciousness, even though you try to avoid it with the distractions of daily life. With years passing by faster and faster, you get your bearings by trying to get an objective overview of life. At first it is more a question of "right and wrong" rather than a question of Truthfulness. *Have I done what's right? Was I a good mother? Was I a good father? Have I been doing my best? Was I honest enough?* and so on. All these questions, based on rightness or wrongness, are the result of the education we've received since birth, but they have nothing to do with our sense of duty to accomplish our purpose in this life while in this physical body.

In reality, it is easy to understand the greater importance of being truthful to that of being right or wrong. Right and wrong are just two points of view that depend upon the value that you place upon them. Instead, Truthfulness should be the foundation of all the questions you ask about everything you have done in your life, the most important being *"Have I been honest with myself?"* To be truthful to yourself is also to realize how much you've lied to yourself, pretending to be someone you're not or having done (or still doing) things which do not correspond to your true nature.

Most people die having accomplished what they envisioned in their mind, but very rarely what they carried in their heart. What aspiration do you have in your heart that hasn't been fulfilled? Have you achieved the inner state of happiness you have been seeking all your life? And if not, why is that? It is because you haven't been honest with yourself. It is never too late to accomplish what you aspire for in this life. You must ask yourself what is going to establish you in the state of everlasting happiness that you've hoped for all your life. With all you have done in your life, if you have yet to find happiness, you certainly won't fulfill your destiny by doing more externally. If you are not yet unconditionally joyous and happy, it is because your happiness and aspiration have sought fulfillment through *doing* rather than *being*. Reflect upon everything you've done and realize that nothing can bring you happiness this way. You cannot *obtain* happiness… you can only *become* happiness.

To achieve a state of pure bliss for the happiness of as many sentient beings as possible is the true reason for existence. It is also your duty! One of the best ways to be happy is to learn the art of being truthful toward oneself. By honestly recognizing the way in which you've lied to yourself by refusing to be honest with yourself, you will immediately provoke the rise of an intense feeling of freedom, simplicity and fulfillment, which is the nature of Truth. To free yourself from all inner conflicts and contradictions is the highest goal of Yoga.

May each of you experience the return to truthfulness with yourself! It is never too late to be truthful!

The Other Dimension of Life

Whether you come to the Meditations at the Ashram in Wasa, travel through the Himalayas in Northern India, or traverse the high plateaus of Tibet, if you listen to the Teachings of great yogis or enlightened ascetic monks, they will tell you the same thing; that you are not what you think you are, but that you are the Supreme Consciousness, the *Atman*. This message serves to wake up the Seeker of Truth so s/he can realize this inner condition as a deluded being.

Most people spend their entire existence enduring a life limited to the small perimeter of their intellectual knowledge. The entire world as they know it is nothing but a projection of what they have learned since birth. They don't know the world and they don't know life; they only know what is in their heads. They do not question the pertinence of their perceptions and ideas about the world. They totally believe that the way they comprehend the world is the only possible, right and true way.

Most human beings live in their intellectual representation of the world. In their reflective world, everything seems so real: pleasure and joy, pain and sadness, acceptance and denial, brief periods of harmony followed by tenacious uncertainty, fear silenced by their opinions, which are no more valid than those of others. Through the mind, they question the nature of the world and they all end up with a certain body of knowledge concerning the outer world. The only thing they will not know when they die is themselves, the very nature of what they *are* beyond their name and form.

It is interesting to hear the most common assertion echoed in the teachings of all great Sages, Saints, Yogis and enlightened Gurus: ***"You are not what you think you are, you are the Supreme Self, the "Atman", and there is no difference between*** *the Atman that you are and God, the Absolute or ultimate Reality."* The remarkable thing is that, no matter where you meet these enlightened Self-Realized Beings along the ages, over thousands and thousands of years, they all denounce the deluding power of the human mind and claim the freeing power of the Supreme Consciousness within us. They share their wisdom with love and help anyone who wants to experience the reality of his or her own true Self, beyond any identification to the body, emotions and opinions. The teaching about realizing one's own true Self beyond the mind is always followed by a rigorous practice, which is a blend of logic, lucidity, pragmatism and intense observation of one's mind.

Once you realize that the mind prevents you from directly perceiving reality, because of its ideas and opinions about everything, then you are able to clearly differentiate between the life colored and deformed by the autonomous activity of your mind, and the other dimension of life as perceived by your consciousness, which is free from the process of mental comparison. Through your mind, you constantly see the life that you know, and not life as it is. Through the consciousness, freed from the mind, you see the reality of life as it is and with this comes a delightful experience of Oneness and Unity with everything. In yoga, to achieve this state of total direct perception of the world and life, without any conflict or contradiction, is called *Ananda* (bliss/felicity), a state in which there are no obstacles between you and the ultimate Reality.

Experiencing this amazing other dimension of life is within reach for anyone who is passionate enough to make the efforts required to control the mind and master the unconscious through a well-understood teaching and a clear practice of meditation. Beyond the apparently tangible experience of life that you believe to be real through your mind, there really exists another overwhelming dimension of Life, and this intense perception immediately liberates you from all suffering and sorrow.

May all of you discover in this life the wonders of the other dimension of Life beyond the mind.

Journey to the Center of your "Self"

If we consider the brevity of a human lifetime and how little we have known about the essence of those who are dear to us that have died, it becomes easier to reflect upon our own situation in this life. What really dies in the people we loved so much and lost? What will really die in our self when we take our last breath? Even if we are not 100% sure about what aspect of us survives when our physical body ceases to function, we can at least assert with absolute certainty that our physical body is going to decompose and disappear forever. So if we know the final destination of our physical body, even though we live as if we were eternal, it becomes very exciting to inquire about the deep feeling that most people have that something in us continues to exist after the definitive collapse of the physical body. This is the true goal of Yoga: to reunite one's waking state of consciousness with one's Pure Consciousness, called the "*Atman*".

The journey towards the Center of oneself in the pursuit of the true Self begins with the fundamental question, "*Who am I?*" This question does not say much at first sight, but look at yourself at this moment in your life, carried away by so many things to do, so many things to think about, and try to reflect upon the very nature of the "*I*" doing all of this. You will easily realize that the "*I*" who is doing what you do is "*you*", but totally identified with your body and your name. With the shape of your body and your name comes the entire story of your life, including everything you want or do not want. And if there is something that you do not want above all, it is to die! But if the "*I*" that you are right now is only "*you*" in terms of your body, your name and your mind, full of imprints coming from the various experiences that you have had in this life, then when your body dies, this physical "*I*" that you have become is going to die and disappear along with it.

Through the unveiling teaching of an awakened spiritual teacher, also called a "Guru", one can readily learn how to differentiate between one's body, name and mind, and the true nature of the "*I*", which does not only exist through the body and the mind, as it survives the separation of the body-mind couple. The true *I am*, *Atman* or *Pure Consciousness* is so subtle that it is never imprisoned within the limitations of the physical body or the mind. The true *I am* or *Atman*, although it sustains the physical body's vitality and reason for being, is in fact never born and therefore can never die.

Through the specific practice of attention, concentration and vigilance, and under the benevolent guidance of an enlightened being, it becomes possible for anyone who has enough interest to quickly differentiate between body, mind and name, and the unlimited Center of Oneself as Pure Consciousness. There is no difference between the Atman and the Divine. If the Atman and the Divine are the Same and Eternal, then in experiencing the *true You*, the *true I,* you will attain Atmic immortality.

May all of you be touched by this precious Knowledge of the Atman, which was directly transmitted to me by my own Adi Guru, this Great Buddha, His Holiness the Lord Hamsah Manarah.

Reincarnation:
What if you have had other lives before this one?

When you approach the High Tradition of Yoga or get closer to Asian Religious philosophy, it seems obvious to believe in the *transmigration of the soul* from one body to another after death.

Considering how different people are in thought and temperament, even those raised in the same family conditions, it is interesting to question why each individual seems to carry their own unique perceptions and reactions to the outer and inner worlds.

In the Buddhist and Hindu traditions, like at the Ashram, reincarnation is not a system of belief but a direct knowledge based upon observation and a specific work of inner inquiry pointing towards what we really are rather than what we *think* we are. What makes each of us so different is our unique way of perceiving the world according to the sensations and impressions we already have about it. For example, you can say that a rose is a rose only because you have already been in contact with roses in the past. You say *"that is a rose"*, not realizing that this assertion is based upon an experience you had in the past. In reality, you don't know this rose *as it is*; you only know the roses you've seen before, and you therefore deduce that you know this rose. How can this rose, which is so unique because it exists for the first time, be exactly the same as all those you've seen before? This is impossible! You don't know what you see; you only know what you have seen. Therefore you don't know the reality *as it is*; you only know *your* reality, which you project upon what really is. Your own mind makes you deform reality and constantly makes you live in your past.

For everything you perceive in this world, be it another

human being, a landscape, a situation or an object, your mind immediately goes deep into your unconscious to compare *what is* with *what was*, a memory of something similar to what you are observing. This comparative process makes you unable to simply and fully evaluate the present moment as it is. Every human being's mind is like a computer trying to recognize reality according to ancient data, making you react according to your past rather than according to reality as it is. For every situation in life, there exists within you a series of memories in the form of emotional impressions and desires that always work as pairs of opposites. There is always what you like and what you dislike or what you want and what you don't want and thereby deny. Even in a newborn, the mother immediately notices that the baby naturally likes certain foods or conditions and dislikes others. Every baby is absolutely different from the start; it does not cry for the same reason or at the same moment as another infant. All these behavioral reactions have been widely studied by highly competent pediatricians, and the result of these studies is impressive: at the moment of our birth we are already psychologically and emotionally different from everyone else. At such an early age, it is not the weight of *this* life that makes us different; rather it is an older kind of weight coming from previous lives encompassing the many painful experiences and emotions we have accumulated, against which we now strive to protect ourselves.

Through the practice of meditation, the gate of the unconscious opens before the Yogi's eyes and from here, neutralizing his or her own past becomes a liberating challenge. For the Yogi, it becomes evident that a human being is not comprised of memories coming only from this life, but from thousands and thousands of impressions coming from far beyond this life. *Why do you really do what you are doing? Do you really do what you want to do or, with a bit of observation, would you conclude that you are constantly "compelled" to do what you are doing, say what you are saying and think what you are ceaselessly think-*

112

ing? Your present situation cannot be explained only through what you have experienced in this life, as there are so many unconscious impressions that trigger you through this long journey you have undertaken on the Path of the Evolution of your own consciousness. Each new incarnation is an attempt to over come this in order to reach a higher level of Oneness with the Ultimate Reality, also called *God, the Divine or the Absolute*.

May this deeper understanding of the principle of reincarnation and the respect cultivated as a result of it, help you to develop the passion for the true *You*, *the Self*, called *the Atman*, beyond your body, your emotions, your mind and the story of this life.

What is the reason for your Existence?

Being so occupied and often even *preoccupied* in our daily lives, it is easy to forget our peculiar position in this world. If you crashed an airplane on a desert island and survived, the first thing you would attempt is to remember who you are, where you came from and where you are now, in order to find your way back to where you belong. Our life is a similar situation, the only difference being that we don't remember who we were before arriving, where we came from, or where we will go after this life. We guess, we hope, we expect, we even convince ourselves of what is going to happen to us after this life, but since nobody really comes back from death to tell us about it, most humans remain obsessed by their mundane and egoistical occupations, acting as if their precarious lives were more important than discovering the reason for existence. Some people think it's impossible to know the answers to these capital questions, and others simply opt for a comforting belief system, hoping they have bet on the best one to secure their future in the after-life.

All of this is not enough for a genuine Seeker of Truth. Seeking for Truth means being determined to experience the reality of one's own True Nature, beyond all appearances of this life in the relative world. Such a Seeker of Truth is called a "*Yogi*". A Yogi is the one seeking a direct experience of the pure Self in this relative world and in the ultimate Reality, beyond time, space, matter, and causality.

It seems a very ambitious goal, but for someone who realizes the impossibility of living any longer without at least trying to find the reason for existence, the Ultimate Goal becomes an amazing inner Adventure in pursuit of one's own true Face.

In order to discover the Reason for Existence, one must first discover the true Nature of their own presence beyond the physical body, beyond their past, beyond their own mind. To do so, the Yogi will constantly remain the impersonal witness of everything s/he can observe and will make a clear distinction between what s/he is as a Conscious Observer and what s/he is able to observe as an object of attention. Since we cannot be what we observe, the attention must be turned toward the very Nature of the Observer through an intense meditation practice. *Who is the One observing this life? Who is the One using this physical body? Who is the One having these emotions and these thoughts?* This observation must continue until the answer becomes a very intimate Experience, more truthful and evident than any intellectual words or definitions.

From there, it becomes clear that the reason for existence is Self-Discovery in order to be able to comprehend not only this relative world, but what sustains it, what exists beyond it, which we often refer to as *God* or *the Absolute*.

This brief reflection on our position in this precarious life can help us realize that there is more than a mundane life to be experienced during this incarnation. This is in fact the reason for our Ashram here in Wasa, since an Ashram is a platform of Self-Transformation through specific Yogic Disciplines with the purpose of drawing closer to what we really are beyond what we think we are. The very Reason for Existence is Self-Realization, also called "Spiritual Liberation" from ignorance and suffering. It is possible. We *can* achieve it. So if we can do it, we *must* do it.

May all of you develop the passion for discovering the very Reason for your own Existence.

Your drop in the ocean of life counts

With all these scary situations happening around the world and the programming of fear willingly spread by the media, it takes more and more courage and lucidity to maintain hope for the future. You may wonder what this humanity is giving birth to. What will be the next step for our individualistic society? Are we falling like the Roman Empire or are we giving birth to another kind of Human Being through these drastic circumstances? Remember that whenever there is destruction, there is always the rise of something new, something more adapted to what is necessary.

"Do not despair, the best is yet to come!" our Spiritual Teacher, His Holiness the Lord Hamsah Manarah, often told us. Out of the apparent chaos, which is organized and spread by residual "karmic demons" comprised of religious fanatics or members of occult financial and political groups trying to control human emotional reactions, will emerge another kind of man: a Conscious Man. It has already begun and this process will not stop but will continue to accelerate.

The more you realize the extent to which the more or less perverted democratic system has been treating you like pawns in a chess game, the more you will aspire to become totally responsible for your life and our human society as an awakened Citizen in your daily life. In other words: *you can do a lot for the world from your present situation in life.*

What does the world need the most at this present time? It needs equilibrium, security and trust. *Equilibrium* means doing what must be done for the benefit of as many people as possible. *Security* means respecting each other and the order of nature. *Trust* means taking care of one another by considering your life as a part of the life of every sentient being around you.

This assertion may look somewhat idealistic, but if it is a necessity, then we better start working on it rather than expecting miracles to happen without any concrete personal effort. By controlling your emotions and reactions, by doing what must be done with peace of mind and a sense of participating in the world's improvement, you will produce a small drop of perfect water in the ocean of life. The situation of the entire world depends only upon the way you are on the inside. Even if you are alone at home, with nobody around you, you are still a part of this world and you have an impact on the whole world through the slightest thought that arises in your head. *The Butterfly Effect* is real; it means that, no matter what you think, say or do, you are changing the course of events of the entire world. The change you bring to the world by being present in it is signed and marked by the very nature of your intention, of your motivation.

If your intentions in life are egoistic, fearful, anxious and worried, then these negative vibrations will color everything they encounter on their way. You hear about explosions in Paris or those that happen every day in Iraq, and you may think that it has nothing to do with you because you live far from there. But these distant acts of terror are the result of a tremendous amount of an accumulated energy of dissatisfaction and hatred. Have you been expressing anger, violence or aggressiveness in your words and actions recently? Then you have contributed to the rise of rage and hatred among all sentient beings of this planet. This lack of balance generates the first dark forces of vibratory pollution in this world.

If your intentions in life are benevolent, selfless, kind and peaceful, then these positive vibrations will color everything they enter in contact with. You will have generated a drop of the perfect energy of harmony and purity and, because you will have become responsible by controlling your own emotions, everyone around you will enjoy your presence. One by one we will bring out the best in everyone around us. We can become the Spreaders of Harmony and Clarity of mind. You want to be happy, we *all* want to be happy; so it is up to us to create the right conditions for a Happy Life. Let's begin now, right where we are!

Your drop in the ocean of life counts so much! Do something good for others a little bit every day: do so willingly, consciously, for no personal reasons. As Yogis (*Beings of Unification*) in this modern age, we must always pay attention to the importance of bringing balance, security and trust to everyone every day. One by one, we will change the world. Yes, it may take some time, maybe a few centuries, but the Human Society will give birth to the New Man and the Conscious Man, who is ready to serve Truth and Universal Love. Do your best and maintain hope... the best is yet to come!

SPIRITUALITY AND RELIGION

From religion to universal Love

Throughout the history of religions, the quest for the Absolute has created a vast spiritual mosaic, composed of all the dogmas developed by humans. However, rather than uniting humanity, religious dogmas have imprisoned them in a huge "Tower of Babel" of spirituality. This very often leads to an inability to communicate, to understand and tolerate each other, and to immerse oneself in the most important of human values: Love.

Wars of religion, terrorist attacks, fanatic assassinations, collective suicides, etc. mark the troubled history of world religions. Yet, well beyond the dogmatic systems which characterize religions, and often oppose them in their foundations, the Religion of the Heart, which advocates Universal Love, is a path worth exploring if one wants to build a human society that is more just, nonviolent and conscious of its interdependence.

How can we, in this planetary "village", introduce innovative moral values, while respecting cultural and religious heritage? By exploring a third way, that of "Unity in diversity." Whatever the Name one gives to God, God remains the Same. His Nature is the Force of Love in which all His Faces unite.

No longer squabble over the different Faces of God. Rather, try to realize His ultimate Nature in yourself, because it is in It that one realizes that God is One and Indivisible. Ultimate Peace and Joy are realized in the One principle of the Divine.

119

May Peace and Joy be with you, as the Divine is always One in you.

Is your religion or your faith the best and truest one?

It is common to believe that because one subscribes to a certain doctrine or religious belief, it is necessarily the best and truest one, while all the others are inferior or less true.

Since we strive at the Ashram to spread a message of tolerance and acceptance concerning all the Faces of God, I would like to share with you a short Buddhist story that was told to me by my own Master, Shri Swami Hamsananda Sarasvati, many decades ago, a story that has really helped me go beyond tolerance through acceptance.

Here is this story:

Several citizens got into a heated argument about God and the different religions, and none could agree upon a common answer. So they came to the Lord Buddha to find out exactly what God looked like.

The Buddha asked His disciples to find a magnificent, large elephant and four blind men. He then brought the blind men to the elephant and told them to find out what the elephant 'looked' like.

The first man touched the elephant's leg and reported that the elephant 'looked' like a pillar. The second man touched the elephant's tummy and said that the elephant was like a wall. The third blind man touched the elephant's ear and said that it was a piece of cloth. The fourth man held the tail and described the elephant as a piece of rope. And all of them plunged into a heated argument about the 'appearance' of the elephant.

The Buddha then asked the citizens: *"The four blind men touched the elephant, but each of them gives a different descrip-*

tion of the animal. Which answer is right?"

"*All of them are right,*" was the reply.

"*Why? Because everyone can only see a part of the elephant. They are not able to see the whole animal. The same applies to God and religions. No one will see Him completely.*" By this parable, the Lord Buddha teaches that we should respect all other legitimate religions and their beliefs.

In the same way, it is essential to enlarge the vision that one has about the Divine and to include in that vision the faith of all those that do not directly share one's own religious belief.

No matter what, it is certain that the merciful Divine is One and the same for all beings. If we belong to God, then God does not belong to us.

May your faith and your prayers join in spirit the faiths and prayers of all men and women united in the principle of Unity and Oneness of God.

Christ and Buddha lived in harmony with those around them

Living with human beings requires a certain art of *adaptation* and *adjustment*. It is unnecessary to create conflict over things that have very little meaning or to contradict others over trifles.

In living with other people, be a servant of the Divine within them. Promote happiness around you and try not to create dissension over small matters. In doing so, your mind will cease to waste its energy, but rather remain bright and joyous. This is one example of certain techniques that promote the positive in your unconscious. On the path of spiritual enlightenment, the life of an aspirant presents many opportunities to adapt and adjust. By learning the art of conforming to situations harmoniously, you become a personality that can move easily and effectively in the world. You are able to bow down to the Divine in others without ever losing your own Divine integrity.

Since you are looking for happiness, then protect it by being the carrier of kindness and attention for others. Forget a little bit about what you want at all costs, and try to care more and more about the needs of those around you.

The true spirit to live and to follow in Christ and Buddha's wake is to practice the Teaching of the Master during the most ordinary daily situations. Do not do what you want, but rather what is needed for the benefit of others. From there, peace and harmony will never leave you, no matter what.

The Unity of all the Faces of the Divine

If you gaze up at the stars and galaxies amidst a clear night while the full Moon shines upon the earth like a giant golden disk, it would be easy for you to reflect upon the fact that we are not alone in the creation, with billions and billions of inhabited planets in existence. We now know that in our galaxy alone exists the possibility of 100 billion inhabited planets. Knowing this easily removes our planet and humanity from the center point of the Universe, let alone the center of the entirety of creation. All of this to say that we know for sure that we are not the only Humanity in the creation and to oppose this assertion is simply irrational. We are not alone!

If you could travel on most of these inhabited planets and spend some time with these different civilizations, you would soon find that each of them believes in the Divine under varying Forms or Names. On each planet also exist several major belief systems, which on Earth are called *religions*. Like on our own planet, these inhabited planets also have a multitude of religions that turn toward the Divine Consciousness, each using different Names of Saints, Sages and Prophets, and each embodying Divine Wisdom and Revelations to define their creed. Since you can expect as many different languages as inhabited planets, you can also expect that the Names used to express God are just as varying and different from ours.

My Spiritual Teacher, H.H the Lord Hamsah Manarah, used to remind us that one should not be deceived by the physical appearance, or the "Face" of the Lord, as there are so many that each humanity favors at least one, if not several. In the history of religions, their quarrels and conflicts were all born from their differentiation between the Faces of God and their false oppositions.

Can we oppose the Light of the Eternal to another Light of the Eternal? It has been done too often by dark forces, which leaned on human weaknesses and the jealousy between religious people. When God takes a body of flesh and matter, He does not limit Himself to the field of a planetary bodily consciousness. Above this Divine Embodiment of God exist different planes of consciousness, which put Him in relation with multiple other Divine Energies projected into matter, such as other Saints, Sages and enlightened Human Beings. These connections don't establish a hierarchy between different Divine Incarnations. Rather, they are each pure manifestations of the Aspiration of the Divine to see that the Principle of Unity of all the Faces of God be respected and introduced into Mankind's heart.

When you turn your heart towards God (*the Divine*), always remember that not far from you exists another Brother or Sister from another Tradition, a Religion other than yours, who is praying in his or her own way to the same God as yours. No matter what Form or Name under which you pray to God, God is One and the Same for all sentient beings.

May Love, Blessing and Unity be among all of us who turn our hearts toward the Unity of the Divine.

May peace and harmony be between the followers of all different Traditions!

Religious Life versus Yogic Life

As soon as you enter this world, you are directly or indirectly walking a Path leading to Self-Discovery. Have you ever wondered about the reason for your existence? Why are you here rather than not being here? What is the meaning of your existence? What are you, beyond your name and human form?

In front of these essential questions, four inner attitudes are possible:

1. You already have a lot to do to solve the daily problems of your life and you are far too busy to consider understanding your life's conditions. You don't believe in much and prefer enjoying life while it lasts. You are a kind of "I will see" person.

2. You have been raised in or discovered a more or less religious way of life. You tend to practice your faith or your hopes according to the time you have available, since you are quite busy solving your daily problems of life.

3. You are a very or even extreme religious person and your religion has given you acceptable and reassuring answers about your existence before, during and after this life. You are certain that your religion is so true that it is "the only One that is right." In such case, it is not that you have proof about the truthfulness of your religion, but your convictions about it satisfy you and leave you without the need to seek out deeper intimate answers. You take sides for your religion!

4. You are or are not a religious person, but you have the conviction that many questions regarding the reason for your existence haven't really been answered. Due to the growth of uncertainties regarding your entrance into life and the afterlife, you need verification through a direct and intimate personal experience. Due to this, you consider yourself a spiritual seeker in need of clues and insights to experience the True Reality of your

own Self and the True Reality of the Divine. You do not seek mere intellectual knowledge, nor do you accept the truth of others as yours; but rather, while respecting all kinds of belief, you pave your own way on the Path of Light. In this process, you aspire to Self-Realization and Self-Connection with the Divine beyond your intellectual abilities and any biases arising from a single point of view.

This fourth category is the one you will find at our Ashram in Wasa. This category of people fulfills the conditions to be called *Yogis* or *Sadhaks* (seekers, Aspirants). Simply adhering to a religious creed, as though belonging to a political party, is not enough for them. The Heart of a Yogi needs more than intellectual convictions, opinions and certitudes. A Yogi, whether from Wasa, BC, Canada or from the High Plateau of Tibet, senses deeply within the heart that there is more to be discovered beyond the intellectual mind's ability to comfort the ego. There are many kinds of Yogis on earth. No matter their tradition of origin, they all seek a direct spiritual experience of Truth (*or Ultimate Reality*) through their Consciousness, which is more than an arbitrary intellectual or emotional conviction.

Being raised as a Christian, I became a Christian Yogi. Discovering the Teaching of the Lord Buddha, I also became a Buddhist Yogi while still remaining in touch with the extraordinary selfless and loving Yogic Life of Jesus. Having been taught by my own Guru, H.H. The Lord Hamsah Manarah, about the Principle of the Unity of the Faces of God, I became a Universal Yogi serving Aspirant Yogis and Seekers from all Traditions.

Within all sincere religious or non-religious Seekers exists a more or less dormant *Yogi*, one who is seeking to Unite with the Ultimate Reality, often called *God* or *the Divine*.

May all of you realize your Divine Nature and merge your Consciousness into Oneness.

CHRISTMAS

You are the Light of the world!

The wisdom expressed by Christ, the Redeemer, is the wisdom of Saints and Sages throughout the world. All religions speak about the same truth, but they express this truth in different ways. When you visit your neighbor's garden in full bloom, you see and appreciate the wonderful flowers that you may not have in your own garden or that you have never seen before. All the religions are like different gardens in bloom, which offer us special divine flowers that we can appreciate with joy.

In this light, let us appreciate two important teachings from Christ:

"You are the Light of the world. A city set on a hill cannot be hidden." (Matt. 5:14)

What enlightens the mind is the intellect. What enlightens the intellect is the Divine Self. This Divine Self is your essential identity. You are not the ego-personality. You are the Light of lights. By discovering this Divine Identity and by awakening to it through prayer, devotion, meditation, wisdom, and virtuous actions, you become like a city at the top of a mountain, a city that cannot be hidden because its divine Light radiates so brightly upon the world.

"People do not light a lamp and put it under a bowl but on a lamp stand, and it gives light to all in the house." (Matthew 5:15)

Since you are the Light of lights and you are in relationship with the world around you, you become a guiding Light, an inspiring Light. The Light of the Divine shines through the mind of a Sage or an awakened Saint, and from their awakened minds, other beings receive the inspiration and are guided.

Be the Light of the Divine, which shines within you and spread this Light to the hearts of all sentient beings!

May the Divine Light within you accompany you all during the Christmas holidays and throughout the New Year.

One of the Greatest Meanings of Christmas

It is said that when Jesus was born in a manger, three kings were led by a star to Jesus' place of birth. In fact, historically they were not kings but three shepherds. One of them, seeing the infant Jesus, observed: *'This child will be a lover of God'*. A second one said: *'No. God will love him.'* The third one said: *'Verily he is God Himself.'*

The true significance of these three statements is that to love God is to be His messenger, to be loved by God is to be a son of God and that the final state is to be one with God. As Jesus said: *"I and my Father are one."* Thus, all persons are messengers of God. This means that they should divinize themselves. When can people call themselves *"Sons of God?"* Begin by recognizing what pure actions are carried out by God; selflessly for the sake of all. There is no trace of self-interest in Him. But everything humans do, say, or think is born out of selfishness. Humanity can describe themselves as *"Sons of God"* only when they are completely free from selfishness and become Godly; when they manifest the qualities of the Father Himself.

Religions arise from the minds of good people who crave to make all of humanity good. They strive to eliminate the evils and cure the malevolent. It is therefore appropriate to celebrate the birthday of Jesus, who felt the need to save mankind and who strove to achieve it. But the celebration must take the form of adherence to the Teachings, loyalty to the principles, practicing the discipline (*Sadhana*) and experiencing the awareness of the Divine that He sought to arouse.

The birthday of Jesus is also the reminder of the constant possibility of God's incarnation in human form in the presence of Holy Men and Women, Saints, and Sages. This must be celebrated by all of humanity, for such embodiments of God belong to the whole human race. They should not be confined to a single spiritual tradition, country or community.

We are not alone and isolated in our world or in the entire creation. God is ceaselessly by our side in human forms to guide us so we can, sooner or later, experience our true nature as "Sons and Daughters" of the Principle of Love and Unity which is the Very Nature of the Divine.

Merry Christmas to all of you! May the New Year bring you closer to bliss!

May you all act selflessly with righteousness to become true Children of God.

For Christmas:
Offer the gift of "freedom" and free everyone you know!

It's not easy to reflect upon the common habit of imprisoning others behind bars of unspoken emotional contracts. No one talks about it, but it is a fact that, behind any relationship between two people, there always exist subtle agreements, which sooner or later become the source of frustrations and disappointments. The mother expects her children to behave according to what she wants. A daughter hopes that her mother will not try to control her. A husband expects his wife and children to recognize his authority. Someone intends to be perfectly understood by their best friend. A son wants his father to be less authoritative and more understanding of his expectations in life, and so on. How many times have you been surprised or shocked by the unexpected attitude of someone who should not have spoken to you the way they did?

No matter what relationship you have with someone, this relationship exists because of implied rules, terms and limits, which must not be broken for the relationship to continue harmoniously. But as you know, human nature is unpredictable. This unpredictability is caused by the unconscious existence of ancient emotions, which can dramatically change the course of an exchange with someone. These emotions can render the one facing you absolutely unrecognizable.

The secret to living in total harmony with everybody you encounter, including those closest to you, is to give them the right to be who they are, because they cannot be otherwise.

Christmas should be a spiritual period of love, kindness, compassion and forgiveness. If, during this wonderful and magical time, you are in conflict with certain people, especially people that you love such as your parents, children or friends, then why don't you return to them the right to be who they are? I call this offering the "gift of freedom". You can always find reasons or excuses for your conflict with others, but it doesn't bring you any good because the sadness of the conflict itself is a constant burden to you. The true reason for any conflict is that we deprive others of their right to be who they are. For example, if someone talks to you in a way that breaks your unspoken contract, remember that you have no control over what they think, say or do.

By giving people the right to be as they are, you immediately position yourself as a quiet observer rather than being the victim of your own emotions.

For Christmas, sincerely free all the people you know from your expectations and grant them the right to be who they are because at this moment, they cannot be different. Everyone evolves and transforms at their own rate and life is too precious to lose one more second in conflict with others, especially those we are supposed to love.

The fantastic World of Santa Claus!

Somewhere within each of us resides the hope for wondrous things to happen in our lives. There was a time when, as a child, you would get carried away by the magic surrounding Christmas, especially through the wonderful presence of Santa Claus. It was a time, not too long ago, when you were eager to believe in the *extraordinary*. If you're honest in reflecting upon it, you will recognize that the closeness you once had with the existence of a world made of pure kindness and total harmony is now missing in your life. Spontaneously believing in the true existence of an extraordinary being in your life such as Santa, was, at the time, as easy as believing that the entire world must somewhere be magical and full of unexpected fantastic surprises.

Through an intense practice of yoga, I have discovered that what you carry within your heart in terms of hope and wonders are in fact fully real and possible on certain planes. What if I could give you proof that even what seems impossible is in fact very possible on certain levels of existence and that you were wrong in ceasing to believe this? What if you could discover that, on a certain plane of existence, Santa Claus, for example, *does* exist for real? Would you not be full of regret in having let yourself be moved away from such a wonderful source of constant and overwhelming happiness?

Then do not despair, as it is never too late! Christmas is coming soon and it is up to you to reopen your heart toward the constant and infinite wonders that can happen to you during this very auspicious time. Before Christmas, why don't you take a few minutes each day to sit quietly and let go of the notion of "possible" or "impossible", which only exists in your head. Instead, reopen your heart to what was once so natural to you: believing that something wonderful is going to happen or be granted to you, not just for Christmas but because of Christmas. Reopen your heart to the Divine Magic, which will sparkle around all of us during Christmas time!

Santa Claus and the Magic of Christmas have not been invented by adults at all. They are simply the result of the limitless openness of the hearts of billions of children who have inhabited this earth. Remember… you were among them not long ago. Jesus said that the Kingdom of God belongs to children and that no one can enter the Kingdom of God without being born again.

By the side of my own Enlightened Guru, I have witnessed my share of genuine miracles in this life, and they keep happening even today at the Ashram. So please, don't think for one minute that the magic of Santa Claus you felt at Christmas time has disappeared or was unreal. If you thought that the magical world of Santa Claus was wonderful, it is because his world was in fact sustained by an even more powerful World, which is the Divine World, the true One… the ultimate One.

Let the Divine Magic of Christmas enlighten your heart again in order that the gift of love be spread to all those you know, those who are dear to you, and above all, those you don't know who need help and assistance right now in this world.

Merry Christmas to each of you! Believe and aspire!

You *do* believe in Santa Claus or something very close to it: Do not deny it!

The very existence of Santa Claus is not as important as whether you *believe in* or *deny* his existence. The day a child loses faith in Santa Claus is also the day he loses faith in *the extraordinary, the unthinkable*, and indeed *the unimaginable* which could happen at any moment. When you think about it, this is a very strange paradox, since, as human beings, everyone of us is constantly striving for a higher degree of happiness, acting as if the next thing will fulfill us forever and thus, no matter our success in this *unimaginable* task, it is the very reason for everything we do. The gift is not happiness. Happiness is the Gift!

No matter how old you are right now, no matter how much you do or don't care about Santa Claus, or how disgruntled you are about life, I'm telling you that you still regret having abandoned the belief in the *Extraordinary*, the *Incredible Unexpected* in your life! And this is an undeniable fact! What wouldn't you give for a miracle in your life right now?

Even those who claim they are "at the end of their rope", when they reflect upon their life, it is clear they are lacking the sparkle for *the impossible, the extraordinary*. In fact, they unconsciously want to be filled with wonder and they too regret having lost their ability to do so.

Let me tell you something about this: the very fact that you are alive right now, no matter what situation you are in, is a miracle in itself, since the very *you* that you are is absolutely unique within the entire creation. Yes! For real, there is nobody like you right now in the entire creation, there has never been someone like you in the past, and nobody will ever be like you again in the future. To emphasize this reality, my Spiritual Teacher once told me that there have never been two identical Zebras since the beginning of time. You are absolutely unique as you are the only one like you, and this is why you are so precious; no matter who you are and where you are. A kind of *magical universal force* has created you with all kinds of elements coming from the stars. Isn't it amazing, indeed *unbelievable*, when you think about it? Why *you* rather than nothing?! You are the very proof of the existence of *the impossible, the unimaginable* and *the unthinkable*; you are a living *miracle* and you don't even see it.

So, please, don't ever say that you have never encountered something that surpasses all logic and pragmatic thought. The reality is that there is more to know than what we know and what we do know is only an infinitesimal fraction of what is left to be discovered. So, open your mind and your heart and feel that you are connected to the existence of *marvels and wonders*, it's just that you simply deny it or don't pay attention to it anymore or enough!

That being said, it is capital to reconnect your mind with the dimension of *wonders and marvels*, since the Force of Life, often called *God* or *the Divine*, is in fact the very origin of your presence at the moment you are reading this article. It would be arrogant and stupid to cut yourself off from wonders and unbelievably good *surprises* which will be directly addressed to you during this life and beyond. Life as you know it is not the only *wonder* you are going to meet. There is an amazing adventure filled with Love and Joyous Evolution that awaits you after this life as well. You will come to see that this is just the beginning!

Believing in this new era is not having blind faith; it is, on the contrary, the act of remaining open to *the unexpected, the unthinkable*, which always happens when least expected, a little bit as if Santa Claus appeared by your fireplace when you thought he'd never come for you or anyone else.

Santa Claus is the Symbol, the Expression of the Omnipotent Divine Grace being attentive to each of us. Deep in your heart, you still hope and believe that something liberating and amazing is going to happen to you, and in this you are right because it always happens; you only need to be patient, as nobody is forgotten on the Path of Light. I have seen my share of *unbelievable* and *incredible* Miracles since I met my Spiritual Master. Everything is possible; in fact, nothing is impossible to an open heart!

Merry Christmas, dear Brothers and Sisters of our Community.

May the New Year 2015 be the proof for each of you that miracles still exist in this changing world filled with hope for the happy "unexpected". The Best is coming; believe and hope without any restrictions.

ABOUT THE AUTHOR

Born in a French Catholic family, the Venerable Gurudev Hamsah Nandatha followed an inner calling from an early age. Through the religious context of His family, at 7 years old He had already recognized Jesus as His first Master and was seeking a living expression of God in this life. From there, His spiritual aspiration continued to grow. At age 14, he read about the important Tibetan Buddhist monk living in France, Lama Gendun Rinpoche, and he asked his mother if he could go visit him. She thought it was an unusual request for a 14-year-old boy, but her son's insistence was such that she agreed. Gurudev packed His tent, backpack and some food, and traveled to the Dhagpo Kagyu Ling Monastery to ask if Lama Gendun would be His Guru.

After spending two weeks living as a Tibetan monk, meditating and listening to Teachings, Gurudev was granted an audience with the highly revered Lama Gendun. After having blessed and initiated Gurudev Hamsah Nandatha, the Lama told Him that He would not be His Master in this life, but assured Him that He would soon find His Master. Lama Gendun Rinpoche then gave Him a necklace, telling Him: "*When you meet your Master, He will ask you for this and you will then know that He is your True Master.*" This is how, two years later, Gurudev Hamsah Nandatha met His Master Shri Swami Hamsananda Saraswati, later known as *His Holiness the Lord Hamsah Manarah*. At their first encounter, His Holiness asked, "*Don't you have something for me?*", referring to the necklace given to Gurudev by Lama Gendun Rinpoche. It was later understood that what linked Lama Gendun Rinpoche to His Holiness the Lord Hamsah Manarah was their direct connection with His Holiness the 16th Gyalwa Karmapa who would later spend time at the Ashram of His Holiness.

Deeply grateful to the Divine for having been reunited with His Guru in this lifetime, Gurudev Hamsah Nandatha diligently followed and practiced the Teaching of His Master, who taught and shaped Him during the next few decades. Having no egoistic spiritual ambitions, being content to simply practice the Teaching of His Master, Gurudev Hamsah Nandatha later realized that He had been progressively and secretly prepared by His Holiness the Lord Hamsah Manarah to continue His Mission in the spirit of sharing the essential Principle of the Unity of all the Faces of the Divine.

With faith and humility, Gurudev Hamsah Nandatha followed the signs given through life's events, constantly trusting the Divine Plan and the instruction of His Guru, also called *His Holiness the Adi Guru Hamsah Manarah*. The relationship between Gurudev Hamsah Nandatha and His Holiness contained all the love and mysticism of the legendary tales of Eastern spirituality. Under the guidance of His Master, through His firm Spiritual Practice, He Himself became Self-Realized and perfectly accomplished in the art of guiding spiritual seekers on the Path of Light.

Seeing His Holiness the Lord Hamsah Manarah for the last time in His body of flesh, Gurudev Hamsah Nandatha directly heard His Guru's last wishes regarding what He would have to do for the Mission of His Master. After the Mahasamadhi (the passing) of His Holiness, Gurudev Hamsah Nandatha then heard the call for guidance from many of His Master's disciples, as they recognized in Him the same enlightened Presence as that of their Master.

Rigorously following the instructions and last wishes of His Master, Gurudev Hamsah Nandatha founded the Adi Vajra

Shambhasalem Ashram (The City of the Diamond Path) at the foothills of the Rockies in British Columbia, where He continues the Mission of His Guru and the delicate work of guiding souls toward a genuine Self-Realization in the rising Golden Age.

An increasing number of people from many countries and all walks of life are now seeking guidance from this humble Spiritual Master dedicated to the Evolution of Souls. Living at His Ashram, Gurudev Hamsah Nandatha is utterly disinterested in any form of popularity or media recognition, as He only guides seekers sincerely committed to their spiritual quest. He says, *"The fully integrated Teaching of the Guru is far more important than the Guru Himself. It is a great blessing to meet one's own Guru. This is why my spiritual duty is to remain very selective with those who accompany me on this journey, as time is as precious for the Guru as it is for the aspirant-disciple. I do not wish to become another spiritual figure shaped by the media. All I want is to accomplish the Divine Plan in all dimensions of this immensely important Incarnation. There are two essential conditions that must never be forgotten for anyone who wishes to become my disciple: first you must be extremely sincere and second you must be 100% One with the universal principle of the Unity of all the Faces of the Divine!"*

Although selective and secluded, Gurudev Hamsah Nandatha warmly welcomes all sincere and committed spiritual seekers. The greater the seeker's sincerity and commitment to achieve the great goal of life, which is Self-Realization, the more the Teaching of Gurudev becomes as sharp and precise as the scalpel of a spiritual surgeon. Gurudev Hamsah Nandatha always adapts his Teachings for the three different types of disciples: *the curious ones, the aspirant disciples, and the true disciples or yogis.* These three levels of seekers correspond to the progressive degrees of aspiration in the achievement of the spiritual goal of life. The Venerable Gurudev Hamsah Nandatha and his Disciples are yogis of this modern age, excelling in the art of adapting their Sadhana to any life circumstances without losing sight of the purpose of life.

ARTICLES CHRONOLOGY

Readers can reach Venerable Gurudev Hamsah Nandatha by sending letters to:

HOLY CITY OF ADI VAJRA SHAMBHASALEM
7060 Columbia River Road
P.O. Box 188
WASA, BC V0B 2K0
CANADA

Or by sending emails to:
International@adivajra.ca

NOTES

NOTES

NOTES

Made in the USA
Charleston, SC
20 June 2016